The Dark Horse

'We might have to sell Tanglewood, Liz, sell Tanglewood and all the horses. Sell everything and leave...'

The trouble with Tanglewood – a financial nightmare, putting the stables and the spirited thoroughbred, Toshak, at risk.

The trouble with Liz – she just won't give up.

Liz and Darren, closer now than ever before, start a bizarre treasure hunt. The stakes are high, and the rewards...

JENNY HUGHES is an established short-story writer whose work has appeared in numerous magazines. Here she has combined her knowledge of horses with her considerable talent for romantic teenage fiction.

Also in this series: A Horse by Any Other Name

THE
DARK HORSE

Jenny Hughes

KENILWORTH PRESS

First published in Great Britain 1994
The Kenilworth Press Limited
Addington, Buckingham, MK18 2JR

British Library Cataloguing in Publication Data
A catalogue record for this book is available from The British Library.

ISBN 1-872082-54-8

Typeset in ITC Bookman 9/12 by
The Kenilworth Press Limited
Printed by Hollen Street Press, Berwick upon Tweed

For Dorothy and William Harris
Without whom...

ONE

WE WERE IN the old hay barn at Tanglewood when Darren told me the terrible news. I've always loved that barn – the wonderful smell of meadow hay, the glowing autumn colour of the stone walls, the way the sun floods in and makes tiny fragments of hay dance in a dusty golden swirl. While I'm going on about it I'll tell you something really embarrassing. I wrote a poem about the barn, six years ago when I was very young – and I actually read the thing to Darren! He's a year older than me so he'd have been about ten and a half, and do you know, he was really good, didn't fall about laughing or take the mickey or anything. That was when I realised he was someone special, and I was right.

Of course I wouldn't tell him stuff like that now; there are some things that are much easier when you're a child, but I bet if I did, he'd still be OK and not tell anyone else. While I'm on about childhood, I will say that one thing that definitely wasn't any easier when I was a kid, was riding.

I had wanted to ride ever since I can remember, but it wasn't until my ninth birthday that I finally wore my parents down and they booked my first lesson at Tanglewood. Apparently I'd been badgering them since I was about three, which seems an awful lot of resistance on their part, but my mum says they always hoped I'd grow out of it. Wanting to ride, I mean. No one in my family has ever had anything to do with horses, and we don't have much money, so you can see why my folks weren't keen to introduce me to that most expensive and time-consuming equine beastie.

Anyway, on this historic ninth birthday I'd finally triumphed, and that's when I met Darren and

Tanglewood. My first lesson with Colin, his dad, who was also the stables' chief instructor, was booked, and I turned up, pale with excitement, in a pair of my brother's jeans (my mum thought they'd 'give more' being two sizes too big), an enormous jumper (to protect me when I fell off, she thought) and bright red wellies. I know! I cringe when I think of it. No hat, you notice, but Colin lent me one that fitted properly and showed me how to adjust the chin strap. I was solemnly fiddling with it when I saw Darren, zooming effortlessly, it seemed to me, round the sand school on Falcon, his grey pony.

I stood at the fence and watched them cantering figures of eight and hopping over low poles and cavaletti. I have never, ever envied anyone so fiercely, and I thought they looked wonderful. Darren looked down and must have seen something of how I was feeling burning out of my nine-year-old eyes. He didn't mock my serious expression or even my odd attire, he just grinned in a friendly fashion and rode over.

'First lesson?' He showed off just a bit, turning sharply and jumping a pole at an angle.

I nodded, too impressed to speak.

'Just listen to everything my dad tells you and you'll be OK.' He looked like a young knight in shining armour sitting up there on his white charger. 'Maybe you'll be joining me soon in the jumping classes.'

I remember sighing with joy at the sheer thought as he moved Falcon expertly away. I wasn't actually smitten with passion for Darren, you understand, I was only nine after all, but the whole Tanglewood thing had already got to me. It was, and is, a beautiful place. The lovely old stone walls of the house and stables seem to grow out of the earth and look as though they're being hugged by the ivy that climbs joyously to each roof.

Oh look out, I'm getting all poetic again. When I feel

really strongly about something I have to put it into words, but people think you're batty if you say stuff, so I write it down instead. I've done that about Toshak – but I'm getting ahead of myself, you haven't even met him yet. Anyway, there I was at Tanglewood, sitting on a horse and feeling I never wanted to be anywhere else or do anything else ever in my life.

I'd like to put in here that I was an absolute natural and was riding like a Cossack in two weeks, but unfortunately that's not the way it was. Like most people it took me quite a while to become even half decent as a rider, and of course I'm still learning now. I was pretty determined at nine, mind you, and by using pocket money, birthday money, Christmas money, in fact any money, I managed to get a lesson with Colin nearly every week. As I got older he let me help in the yard, which meant I mostly followed Darren around and got in his way. Darren was unfailingly patient. Even before seeing my barn poem I think he knew how I felt about Tanglewood and the horses and riding, and how very much I wanted to learn.

When he was about fourteen he shot up suddenly and became much too tall and heavy for Falcon, so one day he and Colin came into the yard with the horsebox and unloaded Toshak. He was a dark bay, almost black, part Thoroughbred about 15.3 hh, totally beautiful, extremely talented – and as mad as a hatter. I thought he was wonderful and was thrilled to bits when Darren let me help with his schooling. Being still quite small and skinny then, I'd ride Falcon, now semi-retired and living happily in one of Tanglewood's lush pastures. He really enjoyed the trip out with me when I accompanied Darren and Tosh on their working hacks across the moor.

It was brilliant: extra riding in return for chores, and the chance to learn more and more. Darren was trying to make an eventer out of Toshak and I got involved in as much of the schooling as I could, some of it quite dull and repetitive, like standing in the school for hours raising poles a notch at a time. But the working hacks were always really exciting. Tosh enjoyed life to the full and gave his all, whether flat schooling in the manège or jumping circuits in the sand school, but his real love was a good pipe-opening gallop across the beautiful moorland that surrounds Tanglewood.

We'd come to realise he was a kind and genuine horse but Darren used to say his brain was in sideways when it came to the great outdoors. Darren was pretty big and strong and had plenty of nerve and know-how, but sometimes it was all he could do to keep control of the wonderful bay horse. Tosh didn't mean to be a pain; he just felt the wind in his face and wanted to gallop and gallop for the sheer joy of it. Little Falcon and I were left way behind when Darren let Tosh have his head, but usually we took the lead, riding squarely in the middle of the slender turf tracks to help keep Toshak literally on the straight and narrow.

We used this system to steady the big bay down so Darren could get him going at a rounded, even pace, toned muscles gleaming under sleek skin, as he dropped his nose, came onto the bit and flowed into a beautiful controlled canter. I used to turn my head and watch the two of them, perfectly attuned, looking like something from a classical equestrian illustration. Darren would make Tosh behave properly in this way before allowing him the treat of a flat-out gallop or a turn round the jumping course.

There were loads of natural jumps on the moor, and by adding a few log piles at strategic points – on the brow of a hill for instance – and incorporating a small quarry, the fairly broad stream, and some ancient stone walling, we'd been able to evolve a pretty respectable cross-country course. Darren and Toshak were absolutely brilliant and flew all the jumps with ease while Falcon and I were a lot slower and more cautious.

It wasn't a case of me being chicken – I absolutely loved it, but Falcon was much older and smaller than the talented Tosh, and he'd never had that sort of scope, even in his hey-day. (Or, as he's a horse, his hay-day!) It was still great fun and I nearly always managed to get the grey pony over everything. I remember taking a ducking in the stream, though, when he first realised I wanted him to jump the logs and land *in* the water – 'No chance, Liz, I'll get my feet wet' – but I didn't get dumped nearly as often as poor Darren in those early Tosh days. At first the horse's brilliance made him very erratic, and while he was perfectly capable of jumping anything and everything, he'd sometimes take fright at the sudden flapping of a bird or the rustle of leaves, and either shy violently or stop dead, giving his rider very little chance of staying put.

Colin was seriously perturbed by some of Toshak's antics and, feeling he'd made a bad buy, kept threatening to sell him on if he didn't settle down. I think I was given the 'escort' duty across the moor because he was worried that one day Tosh would leave Darren out there, injured and alone. In fact, though he was indeed a juvenile nut-case, Toshak had a heart of gold, and always stood looking down with great concern, never attempting to bomb off after they'd parted company.

Darren, like me, loved the horse to death by now (though I don't think he went so far as to write poetry about him), so we developed a mutual conspiracy of silence over the worst falls. I used to carry an emergency repair kit of sponge, safety pins and brush to disguise the worst of the muddied or ripped clothes, and Darren perfected a quick-change routine that an actor would be

11

proud of, once we got back to Tanglewood.

But gradually the work Darren put in began to pay off and, at seven years old, Tosh was well on the way to being a real star. He still had the occasional mad moment, but generally he behaved in a disciplined and well-schooled way, fabulous to ride.

Yep, I'd progressed too, and at the time I'm telling you about I'd grown and filled out a bit, and was actually considered strong and *capable* enough of riding the wonderful bay horse myself. Darren was really, really good about letting me school him, partly I think because I never actually asked, but also because, at nearly sixteen I still looked at Tosh with the same wonder and joy that Darren had seen on my face when I was nine.

So, with Tanglewood and the horses and Darren and Tosh, life just seemed perfect. The crowning moment came at Easter when Colin offered me a job as a full-time working pupil and my parents actually agreed to let me take it! Again, I'd been working on them for what seemed like an eternity. My mum wanted me to go to secretarial college, despite all my pleas and reasoning, but good old Dad had seen that I was deadly serious about making a career with horses and said I wouldn't do better than Tanglewood.

'Colin's known Liz for years and has a good opinion of her,' he argued with Mum. 'He's highly qualified himself and he'll see to it that she takes all the exams.'

'But working out there in all that mud and weather!' Mum only wanted what was best, but one person's dream is another person's nightmare, as I told her.

She couldn't believe I'd find learning to be a secretary nightmarish. 'But I just don't want to work in an office.' I was keeping my cool, ranting and raving doesn't do your case any favours. 'I'm good with horses and I shall love teaching. Tanglewood's business is expanding all the time so there'll be plenty of opportunities for me.'

'She's right.' Dad put in his two penn'orth. 'Colin's just spent a lot of money improving the facilities at the stables. He told me he wants to make it the most comprehensive equestrian centre in the area. He'll need properly trained staff for that and Liz will be right on the spot.'

Between us we won her over. My brother had gone on to university – the brainy devil – and I know she wanted me to have the same opportunity, but we convinced her that my career hopes were centred on horses and that Tanglewood was a kind of equine Oxford or Cambridge. Or possibly both. I couldn't wait to tell Colin, and Darren of course, that I was able to take the offer, and for a few short, glorious weeks everything seemed idyllic. Then came the day when Darren, his dark face unusually worried, called me as I was brushing Toshak down after schooling. 'Liz, when you've finished come on over to the barn. I need to talk.'

I was whistling happily as I removed Tosh's dried sweat, but something in Darren's voice made me stop the tuneless warbling and I gave the big bay a quick cuddle before leaving him with his feed and belting off to the barn. I walked in, breathing the heady scent of meadow hay, and climbed the stout ladder to the top storage level. There were no bales up there – what was left of last year's supply was downstairs now and the attic boards were swept clean waiting for this year's crop.

Darren was sitting, long legs hunched in front of him, looking out across the yard, the paddocks, and to the rolling moorland beyond. He looked sad and vulnerable and I felt my heart give a great twang, of sympathy, I suppose. He looked at me and tried to smile, 'Hi-ya, Liz. Everything OK? Sorry I left you to it tonight.'

'S'all right,' I said cheerfully. 'It's dead easy with the ponies living out, isn't it? I only had the stabled crew to

13

feed and Tosh to rub down a bit. Of course, I hate doing him, as you know.'

He grinned, but turned quickly back to the window as if he didn't know what to say.

'Er, you wanted to see me?' Straight to the point, that's me. 'What about? No problem is there?'

He kept on staring at the view for so long I thought he hadn't heard me. 'Darren?' I said tentatively, feeling really worried by now. He's always completely straight with me, you see.

'My dad's going to speak to you of course,' he said, still without turning to look at me. 'But I wanted to warn you. It's only fair. You've been a good friend and I...I think I owe you that.'

'Warn me? About what?'

'The job. The working pupil thing he offered you a while back. I know you're due to leave school soon and...and...well there's not going to be a job.'

'Not...' I was flabbergasted. 'But why? – What have I done wrong?'

'Nothing. It's not you; it's us. Tanglewood.'

I could barely see his averted face in the fading light but I could have sworn he was almost crying. 'It's...we're...it looks as though Dad and I won't be here, you see,' the words suddenly burst out. 'We might have to sell Tanglewood, Liz, sell Tanglewood and all the horses. Sell everything and leave!'

TWO

I COULDN'T TAKE it in at first. 'Don't be silly.' My voice was sharper than I intended, due to panic I suppose. 'Your dad's put his whole life into the place. And so will you when you've finished college.'

'That was certainly the plan.' Darren got up suddenly and punched his doubled-up fist into the wall. I still couldn't see his face but the tense, angry set of his broad shoulders said it all.

I took a deep breath and tried to calm us down. 'So what's changed? Darren, don't thump the woodwork like that. Sit over here and tell me. Tell me everything.'

He stopped pacing and sat down reluctantly. 'I don't know where to start or how much to say.'

'Start at the beginning and work through to the end,' I said. 'And you know you can say anything, anything at all to me and it won't go further than this barn if that's how you want it.'

He looked at me for the first time and a faint smile lightened his face. 'I know that, Liz. Thanks. I'll tell you what I know. If I've got some of the details wrong it's because I couldn't take it all in when Dad broke the news.'

'If it's as bad as you say I'm going to have the same trouble myself,' I said, trying to ignore the sinking feeling in my stomach.

Darren ran his hand distractedly through his hair. 'It's bad. It's...well, you know we've made a lot of improvements around the place this year – enlarged the manège and laid a new floor, built teaching facilities and extra stabling for competition horses and so on, even down to buying all brand-new jumps for the school?'

'Mmm. It's made a brilliant place even brillianter,' I

said ungrammatically. 'And I know it's all part of the on-going scheme for the equestrian centre, with its teaching and show facilities, examination conditions for people taking advanced qualifications, and so on and so on. Colin was telling my dad all about your plans a couple of months back.'

'I know,' he groaned and held his head in his hands. 'He was so keen once the opportunity was given to him, and so was I, Liz. Dad's been waiting for years to add all these things, but money's never been easy. Tanglewood is a mighty expensive place to run.'

'I can imagine,' I said slowly. 'I suppose I've never really thought about it before. It always seems so perfect and so efficient here but I suppose that's down to the work you and Colin put in, isn't it?'

'Dad's done a seven-day week ever since I can remember,' Darren agreed. 'When we first came he didn't have even a single groom to help. He did the lot – mucking out, grooming, tacking up, taking out hacks, teaching. He's built the business and the staff up gradually so it's run just the way he wants it.'

'So what the heck's gone wrong?' I didn't need him to sing Tanglewood's praises, I was the place's biggest fan, but I needed to *know.*

'It's the money.' Again he wouldn't look at me. 'Dad's in a terrible financial mess and he's blaming himself completely, but I don't think he should. It's...it's Uncle Edward's fault really.'

I blinked. 'You mean the batty old – sorry, I mean Colin's eccentric elderly uncle from Scotland?'

'That's the one,' Darren said grimly. 'He was here a couple of times, you obviously remember. Last time, Dad was telling him about our plans for the future and the old boy said, "Well, do it then." When Dad explained he didn't have the money, Uncle Edward said he'd always admired

16

the hard work we'd put in here and he'd be pleased to finance all the improvements.'

'Coo, just like that!' I said wonderingly. 'I didn't realise he was so rich.'

'He had loads and loads of money. Although he was a batty old coot as you were going to say, he always had a real eye for an investment apparently.'

'That's right, I remember Colin telling me about some rare book his uncle bought for next to nothing years ago and sold for thousands.' I was feeling brighter, all this didn't sound too bad. 'I still don't see the problem.'

'The next bit's where it goes all wrong, and Dad's blaming himself for going ahead. Uncle Edward told him to get going with the work straightaway, and to send him the bills. As you say – just like that. You can see how it was, the money was guaranteed, wasn't it?' He looked at me pleadingly, his dark eyes anxious.

'Course it was,' I said stoutly. 'From what I've heard of him the old 'Unk' was pretty unconventional, but absolutely reliable when it came to keeping his word.'

'*Was* being the operative word,' Darren said gloomily. '*Was* unconventional, *was* reliable.'

'I know he died quite recently, but you didn't say much when it happened...'

'We were stunned. Dad because he was fond of the old boy but me because of the money. Sorry, Liz, I know I should at least pretend to be sorry but I didn't *know* him, only met him two or three times, and I feel really bitter about the chaos he's caused.'

'Well he didn't mean to die,' I pointed out reasonably. 'Was it sudden?'

'Mmm, heart attack, I think. Trouble is it happened before our builders had sent him their bills and he left no instructions about the money he promised to Dad and Tanglewood. He was obviously just going to write a cheque when the accounts came in, but now he's dead...'

'A will!' I said eagerly. 'He must have left a will. It's probably all in there.'

'That's what we thought. There's something called probate that has to be gone through with a will and that takes time. And time was what we didn't have.'

'Why?' I frowned in concentration. 'You mean you had to keep the companies who did the building work waiting for their money?'

'No. Dad would never do that.' Darren was shocked. 'He always pays on the dot – after all, it's someone else's livelihood he says. But to do that he had to borrow a whole pile until Uncle Edward's money came through.'

I relaxed again. It still didn't sound too terrible. 'So it's just a case of waiting for this probate thing?'

'Not any more. We've heard at last what dear old Uncle left us.'

'And?' I prompted. 'How much?'

He took a deep breath. 'No money. Not a penny. He's bequeathed a piece of furniture. A desk.'

There was a short silence. I could hear the small settling noises old buildings make and the sound of my own breathing. 'That's OK,' I said at last. 'It's probably incredibly valuable. Uncle Edward and his clever investments, remember?'

'*I* said that. But Dad got it valued yesterday. It's a nice copy apparently but has no antique value. It's virtually worthless!'

'Oh, no!' Now it was my turn to be shocked. 'He must have thought it was worth something to leave it to your dad like that. It must have been a mistake.'

'A mistake that could cost us Tanglewood.' Darren's voice was harsh with anger. 'To borrow the money Dad had to use this place as security. We can't afford to pay it back now so the bank can claim the property. It's

18

called repossession.'

'Surely the loan can be paid back gradually? What about monthly instalments?' I suggested eagerly. 'If we all work like Trojans and get the business really booming we could...'

'That's what we're going to try of course.' He ran his hands anxiously through his hair again. 'But of course to do that we're going to have to cut back drastically. Staff will have to go and I'll have to be here full time instead of doing the business management course at college.'

'You can always do that once we're straight,' I said, including myself in, as usual. 'And I can do extra hours for no pay and...'

'Liz,' the anger was replaced by gentleness, 'we won't be able to afford you at all. There *is* a slight possibility we might be able to keep Tanglewood but what I told you about your job is a fact.'

'No!' I was near to tears. 'There must be a way round this. I want to help, you've got to let me help.'

He leaned over and ruffled my hair. 'You're a great kid. You always have been.'

'I'm not a kid!' I yelled, infuriated. 'I'm nearly sixteen and I'm not giving up on Tanglewood even if you are.'

'I'm *not* giving up,' he punched the air in frustration. 'I've told you, I'm going to work twenty-four hours a day if that's what it takes to help pay off this loan. My dad was against that, said I had to do the business studies course at college before I started full-time here. He said one of us had to learn how to manage things; he was only capable of towing beginners about on leading reins.'

'You two are acting defeated before you've even tried to fight. If we all stick together...'

'Liz, honestly, it's great of you, but apart from the fact we can't pay anyone's wages now, Dad would hate to get you started on a career only for it to collapse if we don't

19

make it and have to sell Tanglewood.'

'If you say "sell Tanglewood" one more time I'll thump you,' I warned him. 'I can get on one of those employment training schemes where the government pays me and you teach me the job. Between the three of us we'll manage.'

'I didn't know you were such a battler.' He grinned properly for the first time, his eyes crinkling in the way I know so well. 'Come on then, we'll go and talk to Dad and see what he makes of such a campaign leader.'

'Campaign is right. We'll plan it all out,' I said confidently. 'S.O.T. – Save Our Tanglewood. And we'll do it. You'll see!'

When we walked into the house, mind, I didn't feel quite so sure. Colin was sitting at the kitchen table staring into space. I'd never seen him keep still for longer than a minute, so to witness the motionless apathy that had set in was quite a shock.

'Dad, I've told Liz about the money,' Darren's voice was slightly defiant, as if he expected a protest.

But Colin merely turned his head slightly and said, 'Oh yes?' without much interest at all. I looked at him carefully. He and his son were so alike you'd have taken them for brothers if it wasn't for the deep lines around Colin's eyes and the fact that his thick, strong hair that grew in exactly the same way as Darren's, was heavily flecked with grey. They were both tall and powerfully built and both had very dark, expressive eyes.

Today Darren's were bright with suppressed anger but his father's – and I had never seen him like this before – were dull and clouded without a spark in them.

'Colin,' I began, 'Darren told me you probably wouldn't be able to take me on as a working pupil, but there's this training scheme...'

'There's no probably about it.' The man roused himself and turned his attention to me with an obvious effort. 'I'm

20

truly sorry, Liz, but there's absolutely no point in you working here at all, scheme or no scheme. It would be a disastrous start to your career.'

'It's the best possible start,' I said hotly. 'And I *want* to come here, you know that.'

'Just because you like the place is no reason to put up with all the misery we're about to face,' he said abruptly. 'Didn't Darren tell you we're a sinking ship, Liz?'

'Yes, he did, and I told him I'm no rat,' I said, quite neatly I thought. 'I'd never desert Tanglewood and I can't believe you two are even considering it.'

'Have you any idea what we're up against?' Colin threw his hands up helplessly. 'Darren didn't need to start his accountancy schedule to see we're up to our necks!'

'Only our necks?' I said cheekily. 'Then our heads are out, we're still breathing, and you know what they say – where there's life, there's hope.'

'Hark at the girl.' Colin looked in exasperation at his son. 'Has she been going on like this to you?'

'And more.' Darren smiled back at him and I could feel the tension lifting. 'Some of it makes sense, what's more. I've been thinking about it. I know the loan you took out was a short-term one till Uncle Edward's money arrived, but we could change that to a repayment type and pay it off gradually. And if we keep overheads like wages down, and build the business up as Liz says, we could get it paid off.'

'I don't see...' Then Colin frowned as a thought struck him. 'You know, one of our clients is a financial advisor. Maybe I should show him the figures, running costs and so on, and see what he thinks.'

'Great, Dad. That's the first positive thought you've had all day.' I could see the relief on Darren's face. It must have been a nightmare watching his lively, hard-working father slip into this passive despair.

'I still think there's very little chance.' Colin was pacing round the big kitchen much as his son had done in the old barn. 'But Liz is right. We at least have to try.'

'And when you say *we*,' I said firmly, 'it means *me* as well, no arguments!'

'But...' Colin caught my eye and grinned reluctantly. 'Thanks, Liz. I'll have to talk to your parents again but I'll get some advice on the finances first. I warn you, it's going to be hard with just the three of us.'

'Hard work,' I said happily, 'as my dear old granny used to say, never killed anyone. I'm looking forward to it.'

Neither of them looked convinced but I was determined to keep the atmosphere light. Before we'd got Colin talking, the usual cheerful Tanglewood kitchen had been about as welcoming as a plate of cold porridge. And I hate porridge.

'We could make a start by sorting out the stabled horses,' Darren said. 'Thank goodness we're into summer so we don't have to worry about the cold and wet so much.'

'The ponies are fine out in the paddocks and they don't take a lot of cleaning up when we bring them in for the childrens' lessons,' Colin said. 'But Toshak, Cassandra, Kismet and the others ought to stay in at night. I like them turned out for some of the day but...'

'It'll save on bedding, hay and feed if they all live out,' Darren said firmly. 'Sure they'll take more grooming when they come in but we'll have saved time on the mucking out.'

Colin's mouth set in a stubborn line. 'I'm not having my quality horses chucked out in a field like...'

'Uh-oh,' I interrupted quickly. 'First rule of this new regime – no fighting amongst the management.'

Colin raised an eyebrow and looked at me quizzically. 'Is that right? And with this enormous total staff of three

22

who exactly *are* the management?'

'All of us,' I said airily. 'Decisions to be made democratically, if any dispute, a two to one vote in favour will carry it through.'

Colin laughed suddenly, an unexpected sound in the unnaturally quiet house. 'Liz, are you sure about making your career with horses? I think politics or the diplomatic service might be more your thing.'

'Vote for Liz,' Darren agreed. 'Elizabeth Latcham, MP or even PM!'

I worked out what the initials were.

'Nah,' I said. 'I don't want to be a member of parliament or a prime minister. I just want to be Liz TR and Liz TT.'

It was Darren's turn to laugh. 'OK, I give in. What do they stand for – Toshak Raver or something?'

I beamed at them both: 'Terrific Rider and Tanglewood Team of course!'

'Of course,' they both agreed and tried to look as hopeful as they could.

I was genuinely looking forward to working to save Tanglewood from being sold, but I could see one of the hardest parts was going to be keeping these two believing it could be done.

And it could. I just knew it!

THREE

I GOT HOME that evening, my head spinning from all the things I'd learned, and dying, absolutely dying, to talk to someone about them. I'd promised Colin and Darren I wouldn't discuss it with my folks, partly because Colin wanted to get the financial advice before he made any definite plans, and also because he said *he* must be the one to tell them of the changes. I thought that was pretty brave of him but he said it was only fair and he didn't want me putting any pressure on my parents to let me work for him.

'Pressure? Me?' I said, all innocently, and Darren nearly laughed again. I'd really done quite a good job in lightening him up.

Anyway, that meant the only person I could really tell was my friend Sasha, but she was usually out with her boyfriend so I dialled her number without much hope. To my surprise she was in and said she could pop round for a while. Sasha lives just up the road, but I knew she'd do her hair and put on some make-up before leaving the house, just in case anyone saw her.

She smelt lovely when she arrived and I sniffed appreciatively. 'New perfume? Present from Steve, I bet.'

'No, it's my mum's. Steve wouldn't think of buying me presents. I hate men, don't you?'

'No, I don't,' I said, looking in the mirror and wondering why I looked at least two years younger than her when there's actually only three days between us. 'Do I take it that you've had a row with the wonderful Steve?'

'Wonderful! Whoever said he was wonderful?' She flounced her blonde hair around.

'You did. How long can you stay? Because if you're not going to be long I want to tell you my stuff before you start on about your row with Steve'

'I like the way you're so positive that we *have* rowed.' Sasha peered at her reflection. 'I'm not sure about this lipstick. What d'you think?'

'It looks nice on you. I can't wear any, I look such a dope somehow. I'm as tall as you now, but I still look like a little kid who's borrowed her big sister's make-up.'

'You don't practise enough, that's all.' She tweaked her fringe approvingly. 'And a lot of it's because you wear your hair dead flat and tied back most of the time. Get it cut and blow-dry it with loads of mousse.'

'Oh yeah, then stick a hard hat on it and look like a demented poodle in a bonnet.' I flopped down onto my bed and Sasha sat on the dressing-table stool so she could stare at her lipstick a while longer.

'Hard hats are all very well in their place,' she said reprovingly.

'Like on my head!' I said and fell about at my own incredible wit.

She gave me a quelling look. 'Act your age not your shoe size, Elizabeth. Go on, then, tell me this hot news about Tanglewood. Has Darren asked you out at last? Is that why you want to look older? I'll do your hair and make-up.'

'You'll be offering to be bridesmaid next,' I said crossly. 'No, he hasn't asked me out. You know we're just friends. He's really the best friend I've ever had.'

'Don't be daft. *I'm* your best friend, you can't choose Darren.'

'Why not?' I said, all heated. 'Just because he's a boy?'

'Exactly.' Sasha looked at my wall. 'Is that another new rosette?'

'Mmm. Darren let me take Tosh in the clear-round jumping at the riding club last week. He just walked it.'

She made a face. 'You and that wonderful black horse.

25

I'm amazed you didn't pick *him* as your best friend actually.'

'Dark bay, not black,' I corrected. 'You're being quite catty about my little remark, Sash. I was only winding you up anyway. You're the one I wanted to talk to.'

She looked pleased. 'Go on, then, but not too much horsey stuff. I'm not great at it.'

She's right there. We've been friends ever since primary school but once I started riding our paths divided and have never really run on parallel lines since. Sasha came along to Tanglewood a couple of years back to see why I made such a fuss about riding, but everything I loved, she hated. She was scared of the horses, squeaking every time one blew down his nose or stamped a foot, and when she tried mounting she was so stiff with fright she got stuck half way and had to be physically heaved aboard. She moaned about wearing a hat because it ruined her hair, complained she'd broken a nail, and refused point blank to let go of the front of the saddle.

Darren was disgusted with her and refused to take her out, making one of the grooms do it. He said afterwards he couldn't think what I was doing with such a drip of a girl. He's the only boy I've met who preferred me to Sasha – she usually sweeps them off their feet with one bat of her eyelashes – so I was really chuffed. Sasha, in turn, thought Darren was good-looking but stand-offish, and couldn't bear the thought of putting up with all those horrible horses to get near him, so she didn't go to Tanglewood again. (Much to my secret relief.)

Every Monday at school, though, she was much more receptive to hearing my account of the weekend, and lived in hope that Darren would ask me out one day. I tried to tell her we really were just good friends, but she wouldn't have it. In Sasha's eyes that was impossible and she insisted I'd got this terrible crush on Darren – which was quite ridiculous. Well, it was, wasn't it?

Anyway, there she was, all ready to listen, only being Sash she made me sit on the stool while she had a go at my hair 'just as a practice'. I sat there while she brushed out my long, single plait and wondered where to start.

'First of all you must promise, swear faithfully, that you won't tell a soul about this.' I met her eye squarely in the mirror.

She shrugged flippantly. 'Sure.'

'No, *promise!*' I insisted.

She held up her hand and promised so I started telling her about Uncle Edward and the money. To my surprise she was genuinely interested. Not in Tanglewood's future as such, more in the fact that Colin's uncle had promised him so much and yet left him so little.

'They're absolutely sure this desk is worthless?' she asked, backcombing my hair into a wild ball of fuzz.

'Ow,' I said. 'Yes. Colin couldn't believe the first dealer so he had an independent valuation and they both agreed.'

'Extraordinary.' She seemed to be tugging my hair out by the roots. 'Sorry, Liz. So what was this uncle like then? A con man, do you think? Someone who liked to pretend he had money?'

'No, not at all.' My head felt as if she were setting fire to it. 'Don't keep pulling, Sash. Uncle Edward was an eccentric, lived all alone, spent very little, but loved to collect valuable things. His estate was worth a fortune.'

'And yet he left someone who seems to be a favourite nephew, virtually nothing.' She stopped backcombing to my relief.

'That's right.' I tried to turn back to the mirror but she wouldn't let me look yet. 'He visited Colin a couple of times, quite unheard of for him apparently, and was going to finance the new equestrian centre, as I told you.

He was quite straightforward about it, Darren said, only of course he died before he could actually send the money.'

'Straightforward?' Sasha was fishing around in her make-up bag. 'That's a funny thing to say. Your expression or dishy Darren's?'

'Darren's,' I said loftily. 'And less of the dishy.'

She ignored me and started smoothing foundation onto my cheeks.

'Ugh,' I said.

'Don't be such a baby, Liz. Now why should Darren say the uncle was straightforward about it? Was he usually tricky or devious, do you suppose?'

'Well, he was a funny, old-fashioned thing. He liked to set little riddles or quote poetry in Darren's Christmas cards to make him guess what his present was.'

'Did he now?' Sasha looked at me thoughtfully. 'And there always *was* a present, I bet. You know, not a cruel trick with nothing at the end, just a way of making a little boy think hard before he got his gift.'

'Yeah, that kind of thing,' I agreed, wondering what the stuff was she was putting on my eyes. 'But I don't see what point you're making.'

'The point is,' she twirled me round to look in the mirror, 'that there is probably some clue or riddle in this desk he's bequeathed, and the clue will lead Colin to money...or jewels or whatever Uncle Edward's really left him.'

I looked at my reflection and gasped. 'Sasha, that's brilliant!'

She was pleased. 'See, I told you. You're really very pretty now and it's about time you drew attention to it. With your hair all full and tousled like that and your eyes made up to show how big they are...'

'No I didn't mean the beauty treatment,' I said

impatiently. 'I meant the clue idea. It sounds just exactly the sort of thing Uncle Edward *would* do. It hadn't occurred to me – it's rather clever of you when you didn't even know him.'

'Thank you so much.' She was prickly now because I hadn't praised her handiwork. 'Your trouble is you don't think things through properly, you just go crashing about following your emotions rather than your intellect.'

'Ooh, you sound like an Agony Aunt! "Follow your head not your heart, Elizabeth." And *your* trouble, Sasha Gordon, is that you look like a dizzy blonde flake when you've got a brain a university professor would kill for.' I punched her gently. 'And the makeover is terrific – I'm just not ready to look a glamorous twenty-five yet!'

'You don't look twenty-five.' She was OK with me again. 'Ninety-five maybe, but that's all the wrinkles from spending your life in the horrible fresh air.'

'Thanks, pal.' I pretended to hobble round the room on a stick. 'Maybe I'll get some grey streaks put in my hair!'

'Great idea. Well, blonde highlights. I could do it for you. Come round to my house tomorrow.'

'No fear.' I started dragging a brush through my frizzy mop. 'I shall be going to Tanglewood and staying all day. All my exams are finished – I only need to clock in at the end of term.'

'Lucky thing, I've still got two to go,' Sasha grabbed my arm and forcibly removed the brush. 'S'truth, woman, you're pulling it out by the roots. When are you going to sort out this government training course?'

'I'll go and see the careers lot next week. Colin will get the money thing arranged, then I suppose he'll have to give Bill and the others their notice. It will break him up. His way of running things has always been that the staff work *with* him, not just *for* him.'

'He sounds a lovely man.' Sasha sighed dreamily,

brush in mid-air. 'A widower too, and *so* good-looking.'

'Hussy!' I stared at her. 'It's one thing fancying Darren, but his *father?* That's disgusting.'

'I don't fancy Darren. He's yours,' she said, going all dignified. 'And I was thinking of my mum when I said his dad was a handsome man.'

'You're right. He and his son look exactly the same.' I said absent-mindedly, and she pounced immediately.

'See! Hah, I said you were crazy about Darren. All this stuff about not noticing his looks, and being just good friends, and spending all your time with him because of the horses.'

'I don't, and we are, and I do.' I hate talking about my feelings for Darren so I fended her off and changed the subject quickly. 'Anyway stop waffling and tell me more about your desk idea. Surely Colin will have searched just in case there was anything?'

'Maybe he's thick,' she said cheerfully. 'We can't all be as clever as me. You're certainly not, for one.'

'Oh, get you,' I said without rancour, knowing she was quite right. I can't hold a candle to her, not in looks, brains or personality, but of course, I can ride and she can't. And Darren likes me not her. In which case, who cares? 'So,' I continued. 'for the benefit of all us morons, give me an inkling of what we look for.'

'How can I tell without seeing the desk?' She waited, probably expecting me to invite her up to inspect it, but I didn't. For a start it's Colin's desk so he'd have to do the inviting, and anyway, much as I like her, I have to admit I didn't want Sasha at Tanglewood.

'I haven't seen it either,' I hedged, 'but if I do, what sort of thing should I look for?'

Sasha twisted her hair into a bunch on top of her head and thought hard. She still looked great, I noticed.

'Anything the desk contains must *not* be thrown out,'

30

she said. 'Even if it looks like rubbish. Old files, bills, books, even stationery items – anything might hold a clue.'

'OK.' I was impressed. She's so clear-thinking. 'All contents to be checked thoroughly, then. Anything else?'

She looked a bit embarrassed. 'Well, of course, there's always the chance of a secret drawer.'

I hooted. 'Oh yeah? What's that then, or is it a secret?'

'You're so sharp, Liz, I'm scared you might cut yourself. I've read about these old desks. It's quite common for them to have a sort of spring-loaded mechanism tucked away that releases a small drawer. Colin's uncle may have hidden the clue – or even the money – in that sort of hideaway.'

'Wow!' I was even more impressed. 'The things you know! Oh, hang on though, the dealers who looked at the desk say it's a fake. A copy of an antique, so surely it wouldn't have a secret drawer?'

'Depends how good a copy it is.' Sasha looked at her watch. 'Heck, look at the time. I've got to go and I haven't told you about Steve yet.'

'Save it for the weekend.' I removed the last of my mascara and patted the top of her blonde head. 'Thanks for listening to me and for the idea.'

'S'all right. You can always impress darling Darren by pretending you thought of it.' She grinned at me, and I didn't like to own up I'd decided to do just that.

The notion of giving him some hope when everything was looking so black for Tanglewood was a nice, warming one. I thought about it as I drifted off to sleep, imagining the glow in Darren's dark eyes as he thanked me. He was just bending his head towards mine, his mouth almost brushing my cheek, when great waves of slumber rolled in and washed over me.

FOUR

UNFORTUNATELY I DIDN'T dream, which was quite a disappointment. The alarm clock shrilled at six a.m. and I crept out of bed and got dressed in my old working jods with a teeshirt under my jumper. It was going to be a lovely day but the summer was only just beginning and mornings were still cool and sharp. I rode my bike the three miles to Tanglewood. It's mostly uphill and hard work but I'm pretty used to it. To my delight, Bill, the head groom, was still mixing feeds when I arrived, so that meant I could take Toshak his breakfast.

'Early bird, Liz,' Bill commented, his kind, rumpled face beaming at me.

I felt an awful lurch at the thought he'd soon be told that Colin could no longer afford to keep him. Like everyone who worked there, Bill loved Tanglewood and it would break his heart. 'I've finished school, more or less,' my voice was too high and I tried to control it so he wouldn't see I was upset. 'So I thought I'd make the most of it.'

'Getting up at this time of the morning's not everyone's idea of that,' he laughed, and handed me a feed bowl. 'Could it have something to do with a certain dark horse?'

'You don't mind me doing Tosh?' I asked, knowing he was teasing. 'I'll help with the other chores too.'

'I know you will. Go and give him his cuddle first. He loves it as much as you do.'

I walked quickly across the yard where eager heads turned to watch me. 'Morning, Kismet. Morning, Laika. Hello, boys.' I spoke to them all and assured them their food was on its way. They do listen. The only one who wasn't hanging over his stable door was Tosh, but I didn't worry because I knew him so well. I slid the top and bottom bolts and walked into his big, airy loosebox.

Toshak was lying down, stretched luxuriously upon the sweet-smelling straw. Sometimes when you go into his box he's actually snoring (he's such a deep sleeper) and after two happy years here he trusts us all completely and is never bothered by sounds of activity. That day he raised his head and whickered a soft greeting, his velvet muzzle turned towards me. I balanced the bowl on top of his manger and knelt in the straw beside him. Putting my arms right round his neck I cradled his head against me and whispered in his ear.

'Good morning, Toshak. Whatever we have to do I promise you nothing bad will happen to you. We'll look after you somehow, I swear.'

He let me hug him some more, seeming to enjoy the stroking and petting. I gave him one last kiss – I know it's soppy but I bet you do it too – and got up to tip his feed into the clean manger. Tosh got to his feet then, but waited politely until I was leaving the stable before dropping his head appreciatively into the food. He hadn't been this well mannered when he first came to us but the patient, kind lessons had woven their brand of Tanglewood magic on him, combined, I think, with his own naturally sweet nature.

After such an emotional hug I wasn't surprised how hard my heart was thumping – Toshak and Tanglewood and the rest of the horses really did mean everything to me and I was more worried than I'd admit about the outcome of all this. I went back to the feed room to check the daily chart. Colin is very businesslike and keeps an up-to-date record of what each horse is doing throughout each day, so whoever's on duty can see at a glance. Today, I noted, Tosh was being schooled by Darren at eleven, and turned out in Beech Paddock for the few hours up till then.

I checked the others on the chart, then washed the

feed bowls and collected the headcollars for horses going out. Once their feed had been finished in peace, they were checked over, had their feet picked out, then led to the paddocks. Laika, the Arab mare, was first, dancing and flirting with the geldings as I took her across to the small-ish Firtree Paddock. There, a couple of quiet pony mares called their greeting as Laika pranced showily through the gate and cantered over to meet them.

Colin was careful to separate horses who might fight or chase each other around too much and inflict injury. He was a great believer in all the horses having their rest periods out in the natural environment of well-kept fields, especially in the summer when they love to feel the sun on their backs.

Bill had already started mucking out Laika's stable. 'Are you all right to carry on with turning them out?' he asked. 'It lets me get on with this. Mind you,' he winked broadly, 'if you don't want to take Tosh over to his field, just say so, and I'll do it!'

I grinned, told him I'd manage, and went to put Kismet's headcollar on. He's a very greedy chestnut Thoroughbred. Darren says he should have been called 'Eatit'! He was very headshy when Colin got him and although he's a hundred per cent better now I still eased the halter on very gently, crooning to him all the time.

I led him to join four New Forest geldings and a young Dartmoor in the big, shady Birch Field. All the paddocks were surrounded by trees (hence their names) but in case the weather became too severe, either hot, cold, wet or windy, there was a sturdy open-sided shelter that the horses could rest in at any time. Kismet was eager to get to the grass, though, no thought of rest in his mind. He pulled on the lead rope, keen to get into the paddock and took barely two steps inside before dropping his head and tearing busily at the grass. I laughed and patted him, then went back for Tosh.

'Kismet tell you he hadn't been given any breakfast?' Bill enquired, leaning briefly on his pitchfork.

'He certainly dived into the grazing as though he hadn't eaten for a week.' I grinned, but couldn't meet his eye the way I usually did.

'You OK? Not as chirpy as usual today.' His face was crumpled with concern. (Well *more* crumpled, he's got that many furrows.)

'I'm fine,' I said quickly. 'Absolutely fine.'

'If you say so,' he gave a last expert flick to the clean straw and closed the door. 'I would have said the Governor, young Darren *and* yourself were all out of sorts myself, but I'll take your word for it you're all OK.'

I felt terrible and busied myself with Toshak's bridle to hide my burning face. There was no way I could tell Bill the dreadful news that his and the other staff's jobs were threatened. Colin ('the Governor' to everyone at the yard) had already said he wanted to give them the whole story as soon as he knew how the finances stood, but Bill had obviously already noticed something was amiss. I fussed around with Tosh, spending ages picking out his feet, until I heard Bill move further up the yard, then sneaked out quickly so I wouldn't have to talk to him.

I climbed onto a mounting block, took a handful of Toshak's glossy mane and vaulted neatly (I hope!) onto his back. It's not that far to Beech Paddock but I just adore riding Tosh bareback even if it's just for a short distance. Darren always hopped aboard too when he took the horse up there I'd noticed. Colin didn't mind as long as we took the big bay in a proper bridle, and of course wore a hard hat.

I thought I heard Bill approaching so I asked Tosh to move forward and he walked briskly out of the yard, his ears pricked and his stride long and bouncy. He's always like that when you ride him, but like all horses he particularly adores being turned out in the field, and knowing where he was off to, would have quite merrily galloped all the way to Beech Paddock if I'd let him. I didn't, of course. I just maintained the supple, elastic stride of his extended walk. Even at that pace there was no mistaking the fluid power of the horse and I felt the usual great surge of love for him wash over me as we approached the big iron gate.

Beech Paddock is the furthest field from the house and yard, and also the biggest, with one side bordering a long section of a quiet country road and one edged tight against a wooded copse. The only gate is in the fencing abutting Tanglewood, and Colin, or one of his staff, check the perimeter every single day to make sure there's no break or gap where the horses might get out to roam loose on the road or surrounding woodland. It's the nicest of all the extremely nice fields that Tanglewood possesses, but it's also the most remote. I'm telling you all this because these facts turned out to be quite significant in the awful events that happened later.

I slid off Toshak's warm, sleek back and released the heavy bolt on the gate. Colin didn't padlock it because although, as I say, the field is tucked away, the gate can only be approached through Tanglewood's yard, so it's quite safe. I led Tosh through and closed the gate behind us. The bay horse stood patiently and let me give him one more fuss and cuddle, but as soon as I undid the throatlash and eased off the bridle, he wheeled joyously away and cantered, tail high and mane flowing, across the big field. The five other geldings, grouped in a far corner, called their greetings and for a few minutes the six horses cavorted and plunged together, revelling in the freedom of the sweet morning air before they settled happily back to their grazing.

I watched as Tosh rolled ecstatically, his hooves flashing comically, the dark sheen of his coat flecked with dust and pollen. I laughed aloud to see him enjoying the pleasures of simply being alive, and vowed again I'd do everything I could to keep him and all the other horses safe at Tanglewood.

When I got back to the yard, Bill had finished the mucking out and one of the other grooms had arrived to start preparations for the day's lessons and rides.

The yard had that purposeful, organised look it gets when the day's work is getting underway. Usually I pitched in and helped with all the chores, but I was so nervous about letting something slip in front of the already suspicious Bill, I decided to nip straight over to the house and find out the latest news. Darren and one of the dogs were in the kitchen eating breakfast.

'Hi-ya.' He looked a bit pale, I thought, but still trying to be cheerful. 'You're early. Couldn't you sleep either?'

'Not too bad,' I smiled encouragingly. 'We...er...I had a really good idea last night. I thought we could look into it before you start schooling.'

He hesitated. 'I was going to stay out of the way this morning, actually. I don't want to spend much time in the yard till Dad's talked to them all.'

'I'm with you there,' I said with feeling. 'Bill asked me just now what was the matter with us all.'

Darren shot me an anxious glance. 'You didn't tell him?'

'Course not,' I said indignantly. 'He's bound to have noticed you and your dad walking about with faces like wet washing.'

He smiled faintly. 'Yeah, I suppose so. That's why I don't want to go down there yet. Dad's left for the morning, appointments with that financial bod, the bank manager – oh, and some guy called Daccombe.'

'Not Ian Daccombe?' I asked in alarm. 'You know him, that moron who literally beat his poor horse over every jump in that hunter trial I did last year.'

'Can't be, he's only about my age. This bloke must be older, he's interested in buying Dad's Western saddle and some of the driving harness he's collected.'

'But Colin loves that stuff,' I said, surprised. 'Why? – oh, I see, to raise cash.'

'Cash being the commodity we're so short of.' The bitter note in his voice was very apparent. 'So let's hope this Daccombe gives him a good price. Anyway, what's this great idea of yours?'

I plunged into a garbled version of Sasha's 'clue in the desk' theory. I couldn't have phrased it as well as she did because Darren didn't look a bit excited.

'I can't believe there's a secret drawer,' he said, rather disparagingly I thought. 'But you're right, there's a chance the old devil left something in the desk itself. He was very fond of obscure riddles.'

'I remembered that,' I said eagerly. 'Were there papers and things in the desk when you got it? You haven't thrown anything out have you?'

'No,' his mouth was hard. 'I dare say you think Dad and I are pretty thick getting into this sort of muddle, but we're not that stupid.'

I was stung. 'I've never thought anything of the sort,' I said hotly. 'Just stop feeling sorry for yourself and let's at least take a look at the stuff in the desk.'

He shrugged. 'OK. It's through here in Dad's office.'

Still annoyed, I followed him across the hall and into a small study where, in contrast to the modern filing cabinets and severe furniture, stood a pretty, slightly spindly mahogany desk. I tried to shake off my irritation at Darren's prickliness and went straight to it.

FIVE

Darren stood slouched against the wall, watching me as I carefully lifted everything out of the left-hand drawer and placed it on the desk top. I ran my hand all round the interior of the empty drawer, reaching right to the back and crouching down to explore the underneath.

'What exactly are you looking for?' He tried to keep the sullen tone out of his voice. 'A switch or clip or something?'

'No idea,' I admitted. 'I've...um...heard of secret drawers but I don't know how they actually work.'

He took his hands out of his pockets and knelt beside me. 'Surely the two dealers would have found a hidden recess, wouldn't they?'

'Dunno.' I was craning my neck to peer upward. 'If it's really secret maybe they wouldn't.'

We both crawled around prodding and poking but it all seemed smooth and normal. I emptied the right-hand drawer and we did exactly the same, but nothing showed up. We even turned the desk carefully upside down and explored its underneath, spending ages on each join and seam.

'Oh, well.' I gave up, stood up and we turned the desk back up. 'It was worth a try. There must be a clue in the papers and stuff.'

'I had a quick look with Dad,' Darren said. 'But it all looks pretty boring. Old bills, receipts, letters, a few books.'

I flipped rapidly through the left-hand pile. It was just as he said. Some of the bills were dated years ago and the letters were written in faded ink on very thin paper. I started reading one but it was a dull account of some ancient county show. I carefully refolded it and returned it to its envelope, and turned to the other pile. The receipts were slightly more recent and there was a sheaf of newspaper cuttings that, though yellowing, might prove to be interesting.

'We'll have to read these really carefully,' I tapped the cuttings. 'It would be just like your uncle to leave a clue in this kind of form.'

'But what sort of clue are we looking for?' Darren picked up a few clippings. 'There's such a mish-mash. This one's about someone keeping a rare breed of chicken, this one a report on a wonder cure for corns and this is an advert for something called a Morley Bright Detector!'

'Let's see.' I held my hand out for the scrap of newsprint. 'A detector sounds like a clue surely. Oh, it's only something to do with stamp collecting.'

'Must have been one of his hobbies. Two of the books are on philately, look.'

'Philwhataly – oh yeah, like I said, stamp collecting.' I made a clown's face at him and he grinned at last. 'That's better. I was beginning to think you'd never smile again.'

He fiddled around self-consciously with the carving on the front of the desk. 'Sorry, Liz. I know I'm miserable but this is my life we're talking about.'

'And mine,' I reminded him. 'And I know I'm jollying around like it's a game, but I'm deadly serious and I am on your side you know.'

Darren looked directly at me for the first time. 'I know you are and I'm – hey – HEY!'

'What's up?' I followed his incredulous gaze downward. He'd been unthinkingly twiddling with the row of carved flowers that fronted the lip of the desk. Somehow, by twisting the centre of one, he'd released a lock mechanism and a small section of the row had now slid forward a few inches.

'I went all over that bit,' I said in amazement. 'You couldn't see a join or anything.'

'It's incredible.' Darren's long fingers were shaking with excitement. 'Your secret drawer, Liz! I thought you were crackers.'

I slid my hand into the tiny compartment. 'Don't get too excited. It's certainly not big enough to hold a hoard of gold or a wad of banknotes.'

'But it can't be empty surely?' his face was creased with anxiety.

'No, there's a piece of paper.' I scrabbled gently. 'Just a single sheet.' I handed it to him and checked to make sure the little drawer was now empty. 'What does it say, Darren?' (Please, please make it the clue to a million pounds I was silently praying.)

'It's a riddle.' His voice was gruff with excitement. 'You were dead right you clever, clever girl. Uncle Edward's left one of his peculiar poems.'

'Let me see.' I peered at the paper. Uncle Edward had written his address and the date in the top left-hand corner and there, in his lovely old copperplate writing, was this verse:

Colin, you have always known that I'm a real dark horse;
And that I want to leave to you a fine bequest of course;
Tanglewood will make you proud once all your plans are sown;
The fortune's waiting now that you've a dark horse of your own.

'Pooh, don't think much of his poetry. I thought he did a lot of this kind of thing?'

'He did.' Darren's dark eyes were glittering. 'He always gave me a really good Christmas present but I had to guess what it was first. And some of the clues were awful. The old boy liked a pun I think.'

'So what we have to do is find the *dark horse of your own*,' I said. 'What the heck can that be?'

'Look at the date.' Darren pointed a still shaking finger. 'That's just after Uncle Edward came here on a visit – and do you know how I remember that particular month?'

I shook my head, then gasped as realisation dawned. 'Toshak! That's when Colin bought Toshak for you.'

'That's right. I thought *you'd* remember that month too. Tosh was cavorting about in the sand school when Dad was showing Uncle Edward around. The old man was quite impressed with the look of the horse, I know.'

'But what's that to do with the clue?' I frowned, then gasped yet again: '*Dark horse*. That's what Bill calls Toshak – maybe your uncle heard him.'

'Could have done, or just thought of it himself.' Darren was frowning now. 'But I don't see how the money can be in Toshak. He's worth a bit now we've got him going so well, but definitely not in the fortune class.'

I chewed the end of my plait (disgusting habit, I know). 'What about the tack?'

'Solid gold stirrups or a diamond-encrusted bridle? Hardly.' He thumped a fist into his open palm. 'Come on, Darren, *think*. Uncle Edward must have written this clue just after he got back from visiting Tanglewood. That means he hid whatever it is somewhere around the stables. Somewhere that's to do with Toshak.'

'His stable?' I suggested. 'I know it's cleaned out every day, but what about, say, the roof area?'

'Mmm, could be, but I don't see how the old man could have clambered around like that without someone seeing him.'

'Door frame, manger, floor,' I hazarded rapidly. 'Worth a look, do you think?'

'You bet I do!' he marched purposefully towards the door.

'But I thought you were going to keep away from Bill and the others,' I said, trotting rapidly to catch him up.

'I don't mind seeing them *now.*' He turned his head happily. 'Not now we definitely know there's some money. All we have to do is find it and there's no question of Tanglewood closing or the staff being made redundant. You really are brilliant, Liz, with your secret drawer.'

I know this bit's stupid, but once Sasha's idea had been proved right I just couldn't take the credit. It would have been like cheating in an exam or pretending you'd got over a huge jump when you really went round it.

'Um – Darren,' I said, and this time it was me who wouldn't look him in the eye. 'I didn't actually think of it. I didn't think of anything except not letting Tanglewood be sold. It was Sasha. I told her what your uncle was like and she hit straightaway on the idea of a clue or riddle leading to the money. And she was the one who'd heard of secret drawers, not me.'

He gently lifted my chin with his forefinger. 'You're only being modest. Sasha's just a pretty face – she'd never have the brains.'

So he had noticed her pretty face. Feeling suddenly miserable I plunged on. If Darren was going to carry on liking me it had to be the real me.

'I know she's pretty but she's also got plenty of brains. She's going on to sixth form next year and she'll probably get to the same university as my brother. I'm surrounded by cleverclogs, aren't I?'

'Not here you're not.' He gave my arm a friendly squeeze. 'I'm the thicko who received all those clue-bearing Christmas cards, remember, and it didn't occur to me Uncle Edward would do the same thing with his will. And I still think *you're* clever, Liz.'

It was nice he thought so, but I found myself wishing he'd said I was pretty too.

43

'Oh well, let's both try and be clever about solving the clue now we've got it.' I tried to put my emotions firmly out of the way. 'Wouldn't it be wonderful if we could crack it before your dad gets home today?'

His face positively lit up. 'Brilliant! It would be brilliant. I can't tell you how I've hated seeing him the way he is. I know I've been moody and bad-tempered and I'm sorry, Liz, but it's been beyond belief watching him just buckle the way he has.'

'His reaction's quite understandable.' I was trying to put myself in Colin's place, to feel what he must have been feeling. 'Tanglewood is literally everything to him and he's worked his whole life to make it so. He's never owed anyone a penny – I can remember him saying that years ago – so to be suddenly catapulted into a situation where he owes all he's ever worked for, must be like being pole-axed. And to have to admit it to you when you're more than a son to him!'

'You do see things, Liz.' Darren was looking shy and slightly vulnerable again. 'Since Mum died when I was little, Dad's been all things to me, and although we're so alike we sometimes fight, what we mostly are is – well – friends.'

I felt a lump in my throat (horrible expression but when something touches you unexpectedly that's just what happens).

'I know you are, Darren,' I said quickly. 'And I know how hard it is to see friends suffer. So it's down to us to put an end to all your dad's misery.'

Suddenly exuberant he put his strong hands round my waist and twirled me round, lifting my feet clear off the ground.

'I can do anything if you're here,' he said and I felt strangely giddy. It must have been all that spinning.

We made our way to the yard where the grooming and

44

tacking up for the first lesson were well under way. A freelance BHSI came in to take these sessions so Colin's absence wasn't commented on. Bill waved a comradely hand when he saw Darren and got such a broad, cheerful grin in response it must have allayed some of his suspicions.

'Are you going to say anything?' I hissed. 'About the dark horse and so on?'

'I don't think so. We'll hunt round till we find the money or whatever. Dad's got to be the first to be told.' His eyes sparkled again at the thought.

We entered Toshak's stable. It was cool and dark after the bright sunlight. The clean straw bedding had been tossed neatly round the edges of the box and the centre of the floor was swept clean. A well-packed haynet was strung up in readiness for Tosh's return, and his water bucket and manger were scrubbed out. A solidly built, beautifully kept empty stable.

'Where do we start looking?' I was still whispering. Darren grinned at me.

'I can't think,' he admitted in a normal voice. 'It all seems so unlikely once you're actually in the box. The clue *had* to mean Toshak, didn't it? *Now that you've a dark horse of your own* it said. The date coincides with us getting Tosh, and the old man definitely saw him.'

'So, did he actually come into the stable?' I was trying to peer into any cracks or crevices.

'I don't think so. To be honest I used to keep out of the way when Uncle Edward came visiting. He and Dad were close, but I didn't really take to him, despite the gifts. And I didn't like his stupid riddles, even in those days.'

I giggled. 'Careful, you're sounding like a thicko again. If you don't know how long old Unk might have had to hide something, we'll have to assume it was plenty of time and literally take the place apart.'

'I suppose so.' Darren started tapping with his knuckles on the wooden wall partitions. 'If Dad left him alone while he gave a lesson, Uncle Edward could have removed some panelling in the walls, or even hidden something in the roof tiles at a push.'

'Right!' I rolled up my sleeves. 'Let's get down to it.'

SIX

I CAN'T TELL you how long we tapped, prodded, crawled, reached and generally hunted. Darren spent ages unscrewing some screws, hoping to find a space behind the panelling, only to find they were what actually held the wooden batten support onto the old stone of the stable. I had a long, thin tool (a bradawl I think it's called) and went round carefully inserting it into any suspicious-looking cracks in the door and window frames.

We swept the straw bedding from the sides into the middle of the box so I could check any gaps where the walls met the floor. Darren even cautiously inspected the drain, but decided very quickly that even a nutty old uncle would draw the line at stuffing treasure down there. He stood looking around, completely baffled, running his hand through his hair the way he does.

'You're not giving up?' I asked anxiously.

'No, 'course not,' he smiled at me. 'We *know*, we definitely *know* there's something, so we just have to look everywhere possible till we find it.'

'I think we've covered the whole place,' I said. 'Except the roof, of course.'

'Then I'll have to get up there, won't I?' He had a really determined look in his eye. 'I can't believe the old man could have possibly climbed about like that, but I've got to check.'

He went out briefly and returned with a ladder. I steadied the bottom of it and watched him shin neatly to the rafters. He ran the bradawl along a beam, made the most extraordinary noise, and nearly fell off the ladder. He grabbed at the beam with one hand and stood there, swaying slightly and making a horrible choking sound.

'Darren!' I shrieked, not knowing whether to keep hold of the lower rungs or clamber up after him. 'What's happened? What have you found?'

He stopped spluttering and wiped his face all over with a hanky. 'About a hundred years' dirt, dust and mouse droppings,' he said, spitting something out. 'And what didn't go in my eyes went in my mouth.'

'Ugh!' I said, shuddering. 'Are there spiders as well?'

'Just a few.' He carried on prodding, this time keeping his arm extended well away from his face. 'There's no way anyone's been up here in the last ten years, Liz. I'll try the other sides to see if they're any different.'

He nipped swiftly down and stood next to me. His face was streaked with dirt, there were cobwebs in his hair and even his eyelashes were grey with dust. He grinned engagingly at me, his teeth looking very white against his filthy face, and said, 'Good-lookin' kiddie, ain't I?'

I burst out laughing and made a hideous face at him. At that point eight twelve-year-olds who were being instructed in Bill's stable-management class came trooping by the stable. They all stopped at once, of course, and gawped over the door at us. We could hear Bill's voice as he shepherded the dawdlers.

'No need to stop. That's just another stable like the ones I've shown you, mucked out and left clean and tidy, so we can just toss the bed back when the horse is brought in. What's interesting you lot so much?'

His weather-beaten face appeared at the door and he looked in to see one dirt-encrusted Darren with the bradawl, one pink and giggling me with the ladder, and his beautiful straw in the middle of the floor with the haynet, water bucket and manger piled on top (we'd removed them to make treasure-hunting easier). For once in his life Bill was speechless.

'Ah, good morning everyone,' Darren said gravely.

48

'We're just – um – carrying out some essential maintenance work. The stable will be – er – put back to rights as soon as we've finished.'

The children nodded solemnly and moved off to inspect the tack room. Bill hung back for a second 'What essential maintenance is this then? – dusting the bloomin' rafters, are we? I like a clean stable myself but this is ridiculous.'

'Sorry, Bill.' Darren couldn't think what to say. 'We'll be through in a few minutes. I forgot about your class.'

'Hope you haven't forgotten you're schooling Toshak in ten minutes,' Bill said, still looking bemused. 'You've got that big cross-country in two days, remember.'

'Oh Lord.' Darren watched him stump away. 'I didn't realise it was so late. We'll have to carry on with this later.'

'You don't mean we're going to stop searching?' I was flabbergasted.

'We'll have to. I told you, Bill mustn't get wind of our problems. Dad would hate it if we gave the game away, and, let's face it, Bill thinks we're behaving pretty suspiciously. So, let's try and act normal. Could you go and get Tosh, Liz, while I put everything back here and change into my riding gear?'

'Sure thing.' I put up my hand and gingerly removed a cobweb from his eyebrow. 'And don't forget to wash your face!'

He nipped out to return the ladder and I went across to get my hat and Toshak's bridle. Bill was in the tack room showing his class the immaculate rows of well-polished saddles, each properly placed on its rack with bridle and reins hung neatly underneath. I tried to sneak past to get my stuff but Bill, who doesn't miss a trick, gave me a look that clearly said, 'Just what are you two up to?'

I ran up the track to Beech Paddock and called Tosh as

soon as I got to the gate. He was happily grazing right over on the copse side but he raised his lovely head immediately, bless him, and came cantering straight across to me. It's brilliant when they do that, isn't it? None of Tanglewood's horses is hard to catch, though one of the Dartmoors can be quite silly, but Tosh is the only one who dashes to you as if you're the one person in the world he wanted to see. I gave him a big hug and a slightly furry Polo. (I don't always bring him titbits but I just found it in my pocket and he did deserve it.) I slipped his bridle on, brought him out, and climbed on the gate to jump aboard.

Toshak moved wickedly just as I got one leg on and I had to heave and scramble to sit on properly. 'Haybag,' I told him. 'You won't get any more mints if you do that.' He's so clever he probably knew it was an ancient one and there *were* no more, so he didn't care. We trotted quite briskly to the yard with me not bouncing too much. (That's another thing riding bareback does – improves your seat.) We had to go past Bill's little class and they all looked at me, wide-eyed and envious. I know that feeling so well. I smiled at them from the beautiful bay horse's back and hoped they'd be as happy as me.

Everything was perfect again, wasn't it? We were going to find the money, there'd be no question of Tanglewood and the horses being sold and I'd soon be working here full-time. Heaven. I led Tosh into his stable, clean and tidy again now, and began brushing him down ready for the schooling. Darren arrived with the rest of the tack and we started straightaway with the clue business again.

'I think the best thing is to forget it till we've given Tosh some work,' Darren said. 'We know the money is a fact, that's the main thing, and we'll just have to apply ourselves and get down to finding it once we've got time.'

'Good idea. What's the format for Tosh today?'

'Some flat schooling, basic dressage, a few lowish jumps to get that leg change right, then half an hour or so across the moor.'

'Great!' That meant I'd be riding too. 'Who shall I take for that?'

'Kismet's not working till this afternoon, is he? You can take the lead on the gallop track and give Tosh and me a run for our money.' Darren smiled down at me and patted Toshak's neck. 'And as you've been a bit of a treasure yourself, Elizabeth, you can take Tosh in the sand school first for the jumping.'

'Are you sure?' I was thrilled to bits. 'Bill's right, the cross-country course this week is a really big one. Hadn't you better make sure the horse is going right?'

'You're every bit as capable as me.' Darren gave one last adjustment to the girth. 'Anyway, I can sound him out on the moor. I'd let you do that too, but he can still be a bit strong out there.'

'Not 'arf.' I was dying to get started. 'Come on then.'

We led Tosh across to the manège where a beginners' class was just finishing. The riders had all dismounted and they looked in awe as Darren started putting the sleek, deep bay horse through his paces. Toshak's conformation is almost perfect, and with his supple, balanced action, he makes a simple half-pass or turn on the forehand look like an exercise from a lovely ballet. (I don't think Darren would thank me for that description!) Darren was concentrating hard on keeping the horse's interest during the lateral work that Tosh finds frankly boring. Darren is firm but very patient with him and he maintained the impulsion, kept him on the bit and ended with a series of perfect shoulder-ins down the long side, the centre line and off a circle.

I put my hat back on again and wondered briefly what

Darren would think if I turned up one day with my hair tousled and face made up à la Sasha. He's never laughed at me before but I think he'd fall about. Instead, I did up my chin strap, rubbed my cheeks to get some colour and walked over, smiling. Some beauty routine, huh? Anyway, he grinned back so that's what counts. He hopped off Tosh, shortened the stirrups and up I went. Tosh danced about a bit at the change in weight but I didn't want him to think he'd get away with any nonsense just because it was me now.

I made him stand correctly before we moved out to the sand school, which was already set up with a circuit of jumps. They were quite low and I concentrated on changing direction, doing a figure-of-eight course to get Tosh on the correct leg at each turn. He tried to rush the jumps – he loves it so much he would bucket happily over every one with a metre to spare – but it was accuracy and suppleness we were after so I kept his pace down. We were going at a lovely collected canter, following the directions Darren was calling out. It was great, but surprisingly hard work, and I was pleased when we were pronounced satisfactory and could stop.

Jumping classes are OK in a show, 'cos you're only in the ring a few minutes, and I find it hard to concentrate much longer than that. Lucky thing that Toshak has a better brain than me, I guess. Darren had brought a sedate-looking Kismet round for me, all clean and tacked up, and I slid off the dark bay back and swung aboard the bright chestnut one.

'I could get used to this. Horse all ready and brought to me by my personal groom,' I said, showing off.

'Don't get above yourself,' Darren said mildly. 'I just happen to be particularly fond of you today.'

I blushed like mad and hid my face by pretending to fiddle with the girth. He only meant he liked me because of the secret drawer and everything, but it sounded so nice it made me want to cry. (I didn't, though.) Kismet followed demurely as we left Tanglewood, turned right and headed for the open moor. We're incredibly lucky that there's so much land to ride across right on our doorstep. In fact we need to do so little roadwork Colin insists we incorporate it into at least one ride a week to keep the horses used to working in traffic.

Kismet had only had ten minutes or so warming up, so we walked quite a way, then trotted muscle-buildingly uphill before Darren put Tosh into a canter. The big bay pulled immediately but was kept under control, while Kismet stayed effortlessly in his lovely Thoroughbred gait behind them. Darren headed for our jumping lane and we popped through it really nicely, though I could see Tosh was pulling like a train by now.

Most of our carefully placed obstacles were intact but the log piles we'd built had been greatly reduced in height, deliberately pulled apart by riders who didn't fancy anything quite as daunting. You could tell that the logs had been dragged to one side rather than knocked down accidentally, and as usual it irritated Darren like mad. He brought his horse to a halt, holding up his hand so I'd know to stop, and sat glaring down at the scattered pile.

'If people can't jump them as they are, they should leave them alone,' he said crossly. 'We spend half our time out here building decent jumps.'

'It's not *our* moor,' I reminded him. 'And I don't blame people. I'm quite happy to jump this height on Kismet but he'd just duck out if I showed him the stuff you and Tosh like.'

Kismet's a darling to ride, very fast and responsive, but just a bit on the cowardly side.

'Mmm.' Darren was still looking at the spare logs. 'I'm

going to build these back on top anyway, just to give my dark horse a taster for the cross-country.'

'I've never heard you call him that before.' I laughed, and dismounted to help him. 'Bill always corrects the kids and anyone else who calls Tosh "black" by saying he's just dark, but you don't.'

'I'll never call him anything else now we know he's the key to Uncle Edward's money.' Darren was cheerful again. 'I just wish we'd found it before Dad got back. He'll be home soon so there's not much time left now.'

We built up one of the log piles and I walked Kismet through the stream to the other bank so I could watch Darren and Tosh's approach.

They cantered a circle and came at the jump strongly, all the power and impulsion coming from the horse's quarters. They took off perfectly and made a beautifully balanced landing on the soft ground. I clapped loudly and Kismet snorted and nodded his head up and down.

'Thank you, fans.' Darren stood up in his stirrups and blew us a kiss. 'I think this horse has been pretty well behaved so he can have a brisk trip up the gallop track as a reward.'

'Brilliant!' I love that track, particularly on Kismet. He's about twelve now and only had a brief career as a two-year-old racehorse, but he remembers it and loves nothing better than going very, very fast on a springy turf track. I always pretend to be a jockey, crouching in the saddle with my stirrups really short, when I ride him.

Darren and Toshak led the way again, Tosh's flowing canter becoming bouncy and excited as he recognised the wide, uphill stretch of moor we were approaching. 'Ready?' Darren glanced over his shoulder and grinned at my already beaming face. I nodded, and we were flying, flying with the sound of pounding hooves, the rush of sweet air in our faces and the exhilarating feeling of strength and power from the wonderful horses beneath us.

Toshak is part Thoroughbred and incredibly fast, but he's heavier and less streamlined than the specifically-bred-for-it Kismet, and soon I was riding neck and neck with Darren, the two horses stretching every muscle and sinew as they eagerly galloped on. Darren looked across at me. 'We're fitter than you two,' he yelled above the sound of the wind and the horses' thudding feet. 'You can't get past us today.'

'Is that right?' I yelled back and urged Kismet forward, hands, heels and body asking for more speed. He responded with a wonderful surge of power, like a Jaguar going into top gear (the car, I mean, not the big cat). We just managed to overtake and I took great pleasure in deftly moving directly in front so that Darren would get a good faceful of the turf Kismet was kicking up. I heard him start to splutter and I laughed so much I almost couldn't bring the excited chestnut back to canter as we breasted the top of the slope.

He did slow, though, and we came down eventually to walk, then I asked for halt and he turned, sides heaving triumphantly, to watch Darren and Toshak trot up to join us. Darren's face was streaked with mud and bits of grass, and there were blobs of grime from his hat down to his boots.

'Look at you,' I said. 'I thought I told you to wash your face!'

He stuck his tongue out and called me a rude name.

We walked the already cooling horses all the way back so that they were almost dry when we got back to the yard. After untacking them we put their sweat rugs on and left them for some peace and quiet in their stables.

'They're still on a lunch-time feed as they're working,' Darren said, 'though with all the grass they've got I don't think they need it.'

'You're starting to fret about money again,' I said. 'It's all right, remember? *Now that you've a dark horse of your own.* All we have to do is find it.'

'I suppose I'll have to go up in the stable roof again once Tosh is out.' Darren scratched his head absent-mindedly. 'Ugh, I'm all gritty. What with cobwebs, mouse doings, and now thick mud, I'm having a bit of a dirty day. D'you want something to eat, Liz? We can't do anything in the loosebox now and maybe some food will stir our brains into action.'

'Mmm. We might be on the wrong track altogether.' I walked into the big kitchen and stroked a cat. 'This is all very tidy. Your daily's been busy.'

'She's great.' Darren was looking in the fridge. 'Cheese sandwich OK?'

'Nice,' I said. 'So, come on, what other ideas for solving this clue can we come up with?'

He handed me a huge doorstep of bread and cheddar. 'Whatever they are, I hope this sarnie works fast as brain fodder! I think I hear my dad coming back.'

SEVEN

You won't believe it but I munched away like mad, as if by eating quickly I'd get a blinding flash of inspiration and have the riddle all solved as Colin walked in the door. It didn't work like that unfortunately, and all he was greeted with was the unlovely sight of me with a great mouthful of food and a red face from speed-chewing, and Darren with a still mud-spotted face and a half-eaten doorstep in his (thankfully) clean hands.

'Hello, you two.' His voice still held that flat, defeated note. 'Been busy?'

'Incredibly,' Darren's teeth shone through the grime again. 'Sit down, Dad, and brace yourself.'

Colin pulled out a chair and looked at us. Darren fetched Uncle Edward's piece of paper, placed it on the table in front of his father, and told him, swiftly and succinctly, about the secret drawer, the date that matched Toshak's arrival and our subsequent search of the stable.

'*Now that you've a dark horse of your own,*' he quoted. 'See, Dad, it's got to mean Tosh, and it's got to mean that Uncle Edward *did* leave you money...and what's more it's probably been here all the time.'

Colin ran his fingers through his hair and stared, open-mouthed, at the paper. 'It's...it's his handwriting all right,' he said slowly. 'I'm sorry, I can't seem to take this in. Tell me again where you found it. I stayed up all last night going over that desk with a fine-toothed comb.'

We explained about Darren twiddling the carving, and then all trooped into the office so he could demonstrate.

Colin sat down again, very hard. 'I can't believe it,' he kept saying. 'I knew, I just knew Uncle Edward would have wanted to leave me something of value. I was the only person left he thought anything of, but I went over

57

the desk, read everything in it, crawled around it – and found nothing. I'd decided he'd just made a mistake, thought the desk was valuable when in fact it isn't, and that there *was* nothing else.'

'I thought that too,' Darren said. 'And I'd given up. It was Liz who said he must have left a clue, like the ones in the Christmas cards, and Liz who got us looking for a secret drawer.'

'Er – well, it was Sasha really,' I began, but Colin gave me a sudden hug that took both my breath and the words away.

'Liz, you're a wonder! We don't deserve you, do we Darren? You got us back on our feet when we were ready to lie down and admit defeat, and now you've proved my poor old uncle did leave me something after all. What a girl! What a wonderful girl!'

I blushed modestly. 'It's a pity I haven't been wonderful enough to *find* whatever it is he left you.'

Colin shook his head and tried to concentrate. He read the rhyme aloud: '*Colin, you have always known that I'm a real dark horse; And that I want to leave to you a fine bequest of course; Tanglewood will make you proud once all your plans are sown; The fortune's waiting now that you've a dark horse of your own.*' And this date, the date he wrote it, you say it's around the time we got Toshak? I wouldn't know without looking it up.'

'Liz and I knew,' Darren said. 'We spotted it right away and I remembered Uncle Edward had been here just before he wrote the riddle, *and* he saw me riding Tosh that time. He commented on it.'

'Did your uncle call Tosh a dark horse that day?' I asked Colin. He shook his head again. 'I don't think so. He knew nothing about horses, you see. I think he admired Toshak's looks, but I'm pretty sure he would have called him black, not dark. I honestly can't remember. Uncle Edward's visits were always – well – a bit wearing to say the least. I was very, very fond of him and he of me, but we didn't actually have much in common.'

'And I didn't help much; I always kept out of his way,' Darren admitted, looking shamefaced. 'Sorry, Dad.'

'Oh, I don't blame you. You only met him a few times, and he was totally eccentric by then. I remember him as fairly normal from years ago when I was a boy, and he was always very good to me.'

'Did he used to give you cards with riddles in?' I asked with interest. 'All Darren's Christmas presents had clues leading to them he says.'

Colin smiled ruefully. 'It was just one of the dotty ways Uncle got into as he got older. I thought it was pretty harmless and always made Darren co-operate by solving the clues. Trouble is, the old boy obviously thought we enjoyed unravelling his little mysteries. All very well when it's a train set or a Walkman you're looking for, but who'd have thought our whole future would depend on one?'

'It's just the same, only bigger,' I said, not very elegantly. 'We've just got to look at it logically, the way you did with Darren's presents, and the fortune's bound to turn up.'

'There she goes, little Miss Sunshine again.' Darren grinned at me. 'So, come on Dad, be logical.'

'OK.' We'd gone back to the kitchen and Colin started making himself a sandwich. 'For a start, I think you two are on the wrong track with Toshak's stable. There's no way Uncle Edward had the time or the opportunity to hide something there. He spent most of his visit in the house.'

'Is there anything in here that's to do with Tosh then?' I asked. 'You know, a photo or a painting?'

'There are loads of photos,' Darren said, 'but they're mostly in albums – though I think there's one on the wall in the office and another in the hall.'

'There are all his trophies, of course,' Colin put in. 'You two could concentrate on that theme, maybe, while I have another look at the contents of the desk. Now I've got the riddle I might have more idea of what to look for.'

'Right.' Darren pushed his coffee mug away and stood up. 'I've done Tosh's schooling, Dad, so shall we put him back in Beech before we start?'

'Oh, my God!' Colin went quite white. 'Darren, I'm sorry, all this has driven what I did this morning right out of my mind. The opinions of the financial wizards were pretty depressing and I saw Mr Daccombe in a very low mood. He offered me a good price for the Western saddle, which I accepted straightaway. He's quite an astute businessman, I think, and I suppose he realised I must have money problems. Anyway he suddenly asked me if I was interested in selling Tosh.'

'What!?' I screamed. (Nothing to do with me, you might say and you'd be right, but I was so much involved, I'd forgotten that fact.)

'I said no, of course,' Colin said hurriedly. 'But he offered me such an astronomical price I...well, I thought we just had to consider it. I didn't know about the clue then, and all I could think of was getting money together, money that would save Tanglewood.'

Darren had gone very pale. 'You didn't sell him? You didn't say this Daccombe could have him?'

'No, no,' poor Colin looked demented with worry. 'But he kept on and on, saying his son was a very talented rider who needed a really good horse like Toshak. They spotted him last year, and mentioned buying him then, he tells me, but of course that was before I got myself embroiled in all this fiasco – at the time I wouldn't even consider it.'

'Stop blaming yourself for what happened,' Darren said

briskly. 'As Liz says, there's no way anyone would dream that your uncle would pop his clogs *after* he'd told you to go ahead with the work but *before* he'd written the cheque. The main thing is we know now that he *did* leave you enough in the will to make this all right again. All you have to do is tell Mr Daccombe that Toshak is not for sale.'

'And especially not to his beastly son,' I couldn't help putting in. 'He was at my school, Colin, and he's a monster. My mum says his dad has spoilt him since they've become rich. Ian was in the year above me and everyone hated him. He's a bully and a show-off *and* he's cruel to the poor horses his dad's already bought him.'

Colin smacked a hand to his forehead. 'I've been doing really well, haven't I? You're right Darren, we don't even have to consider selling Toshak. Thank goodness we don't – Liz makes the son sound like a cross between a homicidal maniac and a pit bull-terrier!'

He was back to his old bouncy self now he'd seen Uncle Edward's riddle. 'Sorry, Liz,' he smiled at me. 'You sounded so passionate then I'm just taking the mick. I'll phone Mr Daccombe straightaway and tell him not to bring Ian over here this afternoon.'

Darren and I started discussing whereabouts in the house we were going to hunt, but Colin came straight back from his office looking concerned. 'They've already left,' he said. 'Ian Daccombe and his father will be here at any minute so I'll have to get down to the yard before they tell the staff we're thinking of selling Toshak.'

'If Bill hears that he'll be demanding to know the full story,' I said feelingly. 'He's been highly suspicious of Darren and me all morning.'

'I'll meet Daccombe at the gate and fend him off,' Colin put his cap on.

'Tell him you're not selling the Western saddle either,'

61

Darren said. 'Now you know the money's here somewhere you don't need his cash.'

'I can't do that. The saddle deal was just that – a proper transaction – and I can't go back on my word just because my circumstances have changed.' Colin made a face. 'Pity, I really liked that saddle. Still, no use crying over spilt milk, as no doubt Liz's old granny used to say!'

'I dare say she did.' I was still worried. 'But Toshak's different, isn't he? You didn't agree to sell him so there's no question of you having to?'

'Don't fret, Liz.' Colin patted my hand gently. 'There's no way we'll sell Toshak. No way.'

Greatly comforted I watched him leave the house and walk briskly to the main entrance. It was amazing the way that the spring was back in his step. He'd timed it perfectly. By craning my neck at the hall window I could see a long, sleek car pull up beside him. Colin was bending to speak to the driver, obviously Mr Daccombe, and I heaved a sigh of relief that he'd stopped them. But just as I was turning away I saw a figure move stealthily from the back of the car on the passenger side, and begin walking to the yard, unnoticed by Colin, who was still deep in conversation.

'I bet it's that louse Ian,' I said aloud, and called out to Darren who'd started peering behind photos and pictures on the walls. 'Ian Daccombe's sneaked past your dad and is heading for the yard. I'm going to stop him before he reaches Tosh.'

I pulled my boots on and belted down the path, arriving at the stables just as the figure from the car turned the corner into the yard. I recognised him immediately. The expensive leather jacket and trendy, slicked-back hair didn't improve him. It was Ian Daccombe all right, and I was pleased to see the start of surprise he gave when he saw me.

'Can I help?' I said unsmilingly.

'Mmm, I should say you could.' They'd sent him to elocution lessons but his voice still held an unattractive nasal whine. 'I've come to look at a horse. Big black brute he is. Toshak I think they call him.'

I clenched my fists. 'I'm afraid we don't have a horse of that description. There *is* a Toshak, but he's dark bay, not in the least a brute and quite definitely not for sale.'

He scowled. 'How would you know? You're just a stable hand.'

'No, I'm – a friend of the family.' I was amazed at how cool I was being. 'And I assure you, Mr Daccombe, there *is* no horse for sale. You were told that at the gate I believe.'

'You know me?' He looked conceitedly pleased. 'Oh hey, and I know *you*, don't I?' He snapped his fingers like a crummy American actor. 'Lizzie. Elizabeth Latcham, from my old school. Wow, you've come on a bit, haven't you! And very nice too.'

He stepped towards me and a muscular hand grabbed his elbow from behind and spun him round.

'Are you deaf?' Darren obviously wasn't in the mood for niceties. 'Like she said, Tosh isn't for sale. Not today, not tomorrow, not ever. Got it?'

Ian rubbed his elbow furiously and looked as though he'd like to retaliate, but one look at Darren's angry eyes and tensed, hard muscles changed his mind.

'All right, all right,' he muttered.

'And I'll ask you to leave our yard.' Darren seemed quite disappointed he wasn't going to make a fight of it. 'Your father's already turned the car round so what are you doing skulking about here, anyway?'

'Just taking a look,' Ian tried to rally. 'From what I hear you're going to be selling more than just the odd horse. Your business is in trouble – don't try and deny it. If you had any sense you and your dad would take my old man's offer for the horse. It's more than he's worth anyway.'

'We wouldn't sell Tosh to you for a million pounds.' My cool had swiftly and suddenly departed. 'And don't start stupid rumours about Tanglewood just because Colin's sold a bit of spare tack. Your dad put in a big offer for Tosh because you're such a crummy rider you need a wonder horse to get you round a cross-country course.'

'Your looks might have improved but your mouth hasn't.' Ian's face was contorted and ugly. 'We're being generous that's all.'

'You don't know the meaning of the word.' Darren stepped towards him again and he flinched back. 'Liz is right. I remember you now. And she's also right that we wouldn't let you have Toshak if you were the last person...'

'That's enough!' Colin's voice was like a whiplash. 'I will not have my yard used for brawling. Darren, Liz, go about your work and let me escort Mr Daccombe back to his father.'

He turned on his heel and Ian followed him, relieved to be out of Darren's way I think, but as he left the look he shot us was pure, undiluted venom. We walked back to the house in silence. I felt sick and shaky. Although I've got what my mum says is a flash temper, I actually hate rows, and always go trembly if I've been in one.

Also, the look on Ian Daccombe's face had really frightened me. He was used to getting his own way and wasn't going to take being crossed lightly. I glanced at Darren, saw the muscle twitching in his cheek and his tightly clenched fists, and knew he was still full of pent-up anger.

'Let's calm down,' I said. 'We're getting all steamed up when nothing's happened and nothing's going to happen.

64

Ian got his dad to try and buy Tosh because they realised we were short of money and a big offer would tempt us. Well, now we're *not* short, or soon won't be, so that's the end of that.'

'It had better be.' He kicked a stone savagely. 'I'll get that creep if he ever shows his face here again.'

'Phew! Come on, he was only trying to get his hands on a good horse,' I said.

'And on you.' Another stone was sent clattering along the path. 'He looked at you as if he'd like his precious dad to buy you for him too.'

I was stunned. 'Get away, you dope. He hardly remembered me. And I couldn't stand him at school, I told you.'

'He's got loads of money.' Darren's voice was cold and sullen. 'Girls always go for the blokes with money.'

'Well, this girl doesn't.' I said, and punched him, not very gently. 'I didn't go off you when you were penniless, did I?'

'No – ow!' he smiled, and looked at me properly. 'Sorry, Liz. Don't know what came over me. Shall we get back to our dark horse hunt?'

'OK.' I was relieved he'd got over his mood, but puzzled about what had caused it. As Sasha often tells me, I'm pretty slow about some things.

EIGHT

WE SEARCHED REALLY diligently, going painstakingly through every photo album and examining any- and everything that had to do with Toshak.

'It does seem a bit pointless, this,' Darren said, staggering into the kitchen with yet another box of mementos. 'Most of these are from Tosh's successes at shows. And he didn't start winning stuff till we'd had him a good six months.'

'Which is well *after* the time your uncle paid his visit and wrote the clue.' I pushed a pile of photos away in disgust. 'Of course it is. Sasha's right – I just don't think things through.'

'Don't put yourself down,' he said gruffly, '*or* let your peroxide pal do it for you.'

'She'd just love to hear you call her that,' I couldn't help giggling. 'Her hair's mostly natural, I'll have you know.'

'What's that mean – she only wears half a wig?' he mocked, and picked up my plait to tickle my chin with. 'If I pull this hard will it come away in my hand too?'

'Just try it, buster,' I laughed and doubled my fist at him. 'Hey, Darren, if Tosh isn't working any more shall I take him back to Beech? He'll have had his midday feed.'

'That's a good idea. He's got that big course to get round the day after tomorrow so a cushy day won't hurt him. He's as fit as a flea, the grass won't soften him.'

'You carry on here then and I'll take him over.' I stood up and patted his head. 'Yuk, I keep forgetting how mucky you are.'

'I'll wash it while you're gone.' He looked at me rather worriedly. 'You *are* coming back?'

'"Course,' I said. 'I'm determined we're going to find that

elusive treasure. We must be on the wrong track, that's all. I'll try and think of something while I'm riding Tosh.'

'Yeah, me too. Maybe if I stick my head under the tap it'll wash my brains out.' Darren rolled his eyes to make me laugh again. He seemed to be doing all he could to make up for his former bad temper, and I felt all warm and happy as I hopped back aboard the bay horse's back.

We walked somewhat dreamily back to Beech Paddock, me deep in thought about the riddle, and Tosh presumably deep in thought about grazing. It doesn't matter how much fun and feed you give them, grass still remains their number-one treat. I lay on his back for a few minutes with my arms round his neck, smelling the lovely, warm, horsey scent of his skin, before leading him through the gate and letting him go.

This time the other two horses left in the field were very near us, so Tosh merely walked companionably over, touched noses briefly, then got on with his grazing. As I was shutting the gate something in the distance flashed bright in the sun, and I shaded my eyes to squint across the field. It was a bike, leaning on the fence that abutted the road, and I wondered who'd stopped there. I stood on the second top rung of the gate and tried to make out the rider, but the bike moved off.

Just someone stopping for a rest and a drink from their flask, I supposed, and set off back to the house. No wonder I'm so fit. Darren had indeed showered and washed his hair. He is actually very good-looking, as Sash had pointed out.

'Any more bright ideas?' I asked.

'Dad thinks there must be something in one of the books,' Darren said, shaking a handsome trophy vigorously. 'Nothing in here. In the desk there's a book on antiques. We wondered if the "dark horse" reference is a kind of pun about a fake that isn't a fake, if you see what

I mean.'

'No, I don't,' I said bluntly.

Colin came into the kitchen with the book. 'Look,' he said. 'This is a chapter about people who've had what they thought were cheap copies of, say, paintings or sculptures when all the time they were actually priceless originals.'

'You mean the desk?' I was utterly confused. 'You think that, after all, the legacy was just the desk and it's *not* a copy?'

'No, I've had two reputable people quite independently value it. And they weren't trying to cheat me by buying it cheap before you come up with that old one, Liz. Neither of them wanted it.'

'So, what then? What do you think is in the house that could be a "real dark horse" and turn out to be worth a fortune?' I looked round me for inspiration.

Colin shook his head, baffled. 'I don't know. We're not exactly in the stately home bracket, are we? I've bought the odd picture or two since we've been here but I've never been one to spend money on that kind of thing. What I've earned has always been ploughed back into the riding school.'

'That's true.' Darren was racking his brains too. 'What about Uncle Edward, though, Dad? Did he buy you presents too? You never said.'

'Not really.' Colin scratched his head. 'I think he came up with a little ornament once. Otherwise he'd send me a bottle of whisky if he remembered. He was very erratic.'

'Funny thing to give you, an ornament,' I said idly. 'Not the sort of thing an eccentric old bachelor would think of.'

'He wasn't – my God!' Colin stopped and stared at me open-mouthed.

'What?' I said, alarmed. 'What did I say?'

'The ornament!' Colin jumped to his feet. 'I'd forgotten

it completely till now. It was a bronze – a bronze of a horse.'

'A horse...' I said and Darren butted straight in. 'And in bronze! It's got to be a *dark* horse then, hasn't it?'

'Of course!' Colin's face was alight with excitement. 'Now where the...'

We were all on our feet ready to turn the house upside down when the sound of running feet and a loud hammering at the back door brought us straight back to earth. Colin yanked open the door and Wendy, one of the grooms, virtually fell inside.

'Bill sent me,' she gabbled. 'He's got a class and I wanted to run across the field, but he says you'll need to take the Land Rover round the road way.'

'OK. Calm down,' Colin said quietly. 'Tell me what's happened.'

'The fence...the fence is...broken and the horses have got out. They may have gone down the road towards the dual carriageway!'

'The two in Beech Paddock?' Colin was grabbing his cap again when my wail of anguish cut across the room.

'Not two – *three*. I put Toshak back in there ten minutes ago!'

Darren took my hand to quieten me. 'It's OK, Liz.' My fingers were trembling and he kept them folded tight in his hand. 'We'll find him. We'll get them all. They'll be all right.'

We ran out and leapt into the Land Rover parked on the front driveway. Colin let the clutch out with a lurch and we roared away. The country road at the end of Tanglewood's lane is very quiet. It's not a short cut to anywhere so there's hardly any traffic, but a few miles along it joins the horrendously busy dual carriageway that takes you into the Moortown. Colin glanced at my white face.

'It's a safe bet the horses will be heading back this way, Liz, especially if Toshak's leading them. He'll be trying to get back to the yard, not galloping off towards the main road.'

We craned our necks hoping to see the three loose horses coming towards us, but the road ahead was empty. We'd passed the copse and were driving by the perimeter fence of Beech Paddock when I suddenly remembered the bicycle I'd seen.

'There was someone here,' I gasped. 'Just now, when I brought Tosh back. I saw a bike leaning against the fence. Whoever it was could have cut the wire and chased the horses out.'

'Steady now.' Colin sounded as though he were gentling a frightened pony. 'We'll check the fence once we've got the horses safely back. Let's not jump to any conclusions.'

But I could see from the stern set of his jaw that he was grimly wondering what other reason could have caused three peacefully grazing horses to break out and stampede in the opposite direction to home. The Land Rover turned the next corner and Darren nearly crushed all the bones in my hand which he was still holding.

'Straight ahead! Grass verge on the right. That's Drummer!'

He was right. The round, piebald rump belonged unmistakably to one of our oldest geldings, quietly cropping grass at the side of the road. He was very steady and placid by nature and had obviously decided that the wild, free life was not for him. Colin slowed down and Wendy jumped out holding a headcollar behind her back. She caught him easily and was slipping the headcollar on as we roared away. My heart was thumping like a pneumatic drill. Where was Toshak, and the other horse, the young and slightly scatty Malachi? It was less than a mile now to the dual carriageway and the two of them had not been sidetracked by the roadside grass like Drummer.

Colin raced on and suddenly, just ahead, we could see two horses both cantering, heads high and tails streaming, on the grass to our left. And a few hundred yards further was the junction that would take them straight across the busiest section of road in the area.

'Drive just beyond them, Dad, and try to block their way.' Darren had finally let go of my hand and was grabbing the door handle. 'I'll jump out and turn them.'

It was our only chance. We were too close to the dual carriageway to stop and catch them gently. The Land Rover raced past the swiftly moving horses and I was flung to the floor as Colin slewed it sharply to the left. Darren leapt out before we'd come to a halt and half fell as he landed. But he jumped to his feet and swung one arm wildly.

'Hey up, hey up. Get back! Go-ooo-oo on!' he yelled loudly as the two bolting horses veered uncertainly into the road to get past the Land Rover. Tosh snorted and wheeled, turning away from the lethal road junction and Malachi followed. I stood beside Darren and we called Tosh's name.

'Whoa boy. Steady, Toshak. Steady.'

We didn't have much hope that we'd be able to stop him in his panic-stricken dash, but to my joy he slowed at the sound of our voices and eventually came to a halt some way down the road. Malachi thundered on for a while, but realising he was alone, he too stopped and we were able to approach them quietly. I slipped Tosh's headcollar over his dark ears and kissed his soft muzzle gratefully.

'I know you want to cuddle Tosh,' Darren's voice sounded odd. 'But could you possibly leave him with me and go and catch Malachi?'

71

'All right.' I glanced quickly at his ashen face. 'Darren?'

'Please, Liz!'

I did as he asked, and although Mal shied a bit and took a few half-hearted steps to avoid me, I think he was glad to be caught. Colin waited till we were back in control, then drove quietly past, and as we approached Beech Paddock's fence we could see him there, closely examining a portion of it.

'You were right, Liz.' He held up the wire for me to see. 'Cut. Deliberately snapped clean in two.'

Wendy was beside him, holding the piebald gelding, and to my surprise there were tears rolling down her face.

'What's the matter? Is Drummer hurt?' I asked in alarm.

'No, he's fine,' Colin said shortly. 'Here's Darren now. We'll have to take the horses past the copse and through the main gate into the yard. Tosh had better stay in, but the other two can go in Birch for now if they're unhurt.'

'But why would anyone want...' I broke off as Darren sagged suddenly against Toshak's shoulder. 'What's the matter with everyone? Wendy's crying and Darren looks as if he's going to pass out.'

Colin's head came up sharply. 'What's – good God, you're hurt!'

'It's my arm,' Darren grunted in pain as he tried to move it. 'I think I broke it when I went crashing out of the Land Rover just now.'

'Liz, you and Wendy get the horses back. I'm taking him straight to hospital.'

Dumbly I got hold of Tosh's lead rope and watched in disbelief as Colin helped his son carefully into the passenger seat. They roared off and I led the way with the deep bay and the young palomino, as a still sniffing Wendy followed with Drummer.

NINE

I SUPPOSE I was in a state of shock. I know I helped check all three horses thoroughly, but it was as if I was on autopilot or something. When Bill finished his lessons he came straight into Toshak's stable, obviously to find out just what was going on, but he took one look at my white, strained face and softened visibly.

'He's perfectly all right.' He slapped Tosh's shining rump affectionately. 'Just a bit of a jaunt out to him, so let's leave him with his haynet and get you sorted out, young lady.'

I let him lead me across to the staff rest room, where he sat me down and plonked a big mug of steaming hot tea in front of me. 'I don't think it's the fashionable treatment nowadays,' he said cheerfully, 'but knock it back anyway and you'll feel better.'

I took a cautious sip and asked 'Where's Wendy? Is she all right?'

'No, she's in a worse state than you. Blaming herself for the horses getting out. Keeps blubbing they could have been killed.'

'She's right, they could.' I shuddered and took another gulp of the sweet tea. 'But why does she say it's her fault?'

'I haven't got the whole story, not by a long chalk, but it seems she's acquainted with one Ian Daccombe.'

I gasped, and he looked at me curiously. 'She says she met him in the road outside, when she was bringing Talisman back from the moor. He was on a bike and he asked her where that dark horse of ours was kept. Wendy says she wouldn't tell him at first, couldn't think what it was to do with him, but he sweet-talked her into believing he wanted to take a photo of the horse to persuade his father to buy him.'

'What a liar!' I burst out. 'He'd already talked his dad into making an offer which Colin and Darren turned down. There wasn't any question of him needing a photograph.'

'Like me,' Bill said patiently, 'Wendy had not been informed of any of what you've just said. But, unlike me, she didn't think there was anything suspicious in the lad wanting to see Toshak, so she told him the dark one would be either in his stable or in Beech Paddock. So off he pedalled and into the yard went Wendy.'

'Not her fault then.' I tried to push away the picture of Darren's pain-racked face. 'Ian was getting back at us for chasing him off and refusing to sell Toshak.'

'You sound very sure of that.' Bill cocked his head to one side.

'It could only be him. He must have cycled round the road and hung about till he saw Tosh being turned out in Beech. I caught a glimpse of a bike when I took the horse over there, but of course I didn't dream it belonged to Dastardly Daccombe. He was in his father's car when I saw him.'

'Mmm. I'd like to know what made him and his dad think Toshak was for sale in the first place,' Bill said shrewdly. 'But perhaps I'd better have a chat with the Governor about that.'

'Sorry, Bill.' I was near to tears again, it had all been so awful. 'Colin wants to talk to you I know, so I don't want to say anything before he has a word. It's been – well, anyway, he'll tell you it's all going to be fine now.'

'Glad to hear it.' Bill did his crumple-faced grin at me. 'I can't do with weeping females about the place.'

'I didn't actually weep,' I said with dignity. 'It was only poor Wendy...'

A thought struck my slow brain. 'Hey, if she just

74

directed Ian to Beech Paddock's fence, but went into the yard herself, how come she discovered the horses were out so quickly? She couldn't see them from here.'

'She walked over to Beech hoping to see the young man and his camera, and perhaps have another little chat.' Bill winked at me solemnly. 'Wendy doesn't get chatted up much, and she was – flattered.'

'She *must* be hard up,' I said involuntarily. 'No, that's a mean thing to say. She might know him slightly but she can't know what a foul creep he is. Still, at least she saw him cut the fence and drive the horses out onto the road towards the dual carriageway. We couldn't understand why they were headed in that direction, but if Wendy actually saw Ian chasing them out we can tell the police and...'

'But she didn't,' Bill cut in. 'She told me when she got to the paddock there was no one there, no horses, no bike, no nothing. So we can't *prove* it was this Ian Daccombe.'

'But it's obvious,' I said hotly.

'Of course it is, but if he's the sort of person you say, he'll brazen it out, won't he? The Governor will sort it all out when they get back from the hospital anyway. You just finish your tea and stop worrying about it for a while.'

Easy for him to say, I thought, but took another obedient sip from my mug. Afterwards I got on with some of the day-to-day chores – grooming, tacking up and helping with lessons – so the time should have flown, but it seemed an eternity till I heard Colin's voice. Darren was back too, still quite pale but looking better, despite the gleaming white plaster cast on his arm.

'It *is* broken then?' I touched his hand gently.

'Yes, 'fraid so. Not much good at the old heroics, am I?' He smiled at me, his eyes crinkling warmly.

'You were amazing!' I said. 'If you hadn't thrown your-self out of the Land Rover like that, Tosh and Malachi would be...'

'Oh, 's'truth. Don't set her thinking about what could have happened.' Bill raised his hands in mock despair. 'One girlie at a time having the vapours is enough for me!'

'You mean Wendy.' Colin said, his voice flat. 'She told me straightaway what she'd said to young Daccombe. With the fright we'd just had, I was probably too harsh with her. She genuinely didn't know what he had in mind, and she raised the alarm pretty quick once she found out. I'll go and talk to her.'

'Right you are.' Bill started to walk away.

'Oh – and Bill,' Colin sounded oddly diffident. 'If you can spare ten minutes or so I'd like a chat with you, please.'

'Right again.' The head groom's face was expression-less, but I knew he was glad he was being put in the picture at last.

Darren and I looked in on Toshak, who was pulling contentedly at his haynet.

'He doesn't look a bit bothered,' Darren said, scratch-ing him affectionately between his ears.

Tosh nudged him in agreement, rolling his eyes at the strange, gleaming plaster.

'He's lucky,' I said with feeling. 'I'm still getting the horrors thinking what might have happened if the horses had reached that dual carriageway. You're reporting Ian Daccombe to the police, of course?'

'There we have yet another problem,' Darren bolted the stable door securely. 'Let's go back to the house, Liz.'

It seemed quite natural that he should tuck his unin-jured arm through mine as we walked, and despite all the anxieties crowding my mind – the elusive treasure, the fiendish Ian and how to protect Tosh from him – I was aware of a glow of happiness and knew I'd have to write down how I was feeling. Whether I'd be able to find the words was another thing. Anyway, glow or not, there was an awful lot to sort out.

'So why is getting that scumbag Ian locked up a problem?' I demanded, filling up the kettle and rinsing out our lunch-time coffee cups.

Darren laughed and sat down, resting his broken arm in its sling on the kitchen table. 'You sound so fierce when you say his name,' he said.

'You weren't exactly gentle with him yourself earlier on,' I retorted. 'I thought you were going to punch him one.'

'I'd have loved to. Even more so now, but Dad's spoken to Mr Daccombe and he says we can't prove a thing, so we have to leave it.'

'Leave it!' I slammed a cup down and stared at him. 'But Wendy – he spoke to Wendy. He told her a cock-and-bull story about taking Tosh's photograph and...'

'I know, I know,' he rested his head wearily on the back of the chair. 'But she didn't see him cut the fence, did she? Dad spoke to his father, told him exactly what Ian had said to Wendy, but Daccombe said his son would never do such a thing to the horses. He actually called Ian into the room, and Dad says he just looked them both straight in the eye and denied going anywhere near Beech Paddock.'

'But that's rubbish! I saw his bike.'

'You saw *a* bike,' Darren reminded me. 'Dad couldn't believe Ian had the nerve to deny everything. His story was that he was just chatting Wendy up and that the photo excuse was the first thing that came into his head. Dad was so mad he told me he wished he'd lied and told Daccombe his precious son had actually been *seen* chasing our horses out onto the road, but you know how

77

honest my dear old pop is.'

'I do know. And I also know that Ian 'Foulface' Daccombe is exactly the opposite. He's managed to hide the fact from his dad, that's obvious. Even the most doting father wouldn't tolerate what Ian did today.'

'And we'd be doing his father a good turn if we could show him the sort of son Ian's turning out to be.' Darren drank some of his coffee. 'But as the swine has achieved what he set out to do, though not in the way he intended, I don't suppose our paths will cross for some time.'

'What do you mean, achieved what he set out to do?' I said, puzzled. 'Surely his intention was to get back at us by having Tosh injured?'

'Well, yes, that was partly the plan, no doubt. But now he's put me out of action, that at least leaves the way clear for him to star in the big cross-country, doesn't it? He's got a pretty good horse of his own, and without Toshak competing against him he's almost bound to win. He practically boasted of doing just that in front of my dad.'

'Oh, Lord.' I sat back in disgust. 'Hey, you don't think he'll have another go at Tosh so the pair of you don't beat him when you're fit again?'

'Don't start worrying about that yet.' Darren patted my shoulder with his good hand. 'I think even Ian Daccombe is smart enough to stay clear of here for a while. I really hate to think of him winning on Thursday, though. It bugs me more than I can say.'

'Your dad!' I said excitedly. 'Can't Colin take Tosh round? I know he doesn't ride him often but they're both brilliant and...'

'Good idea, except for one thing – Dad happens to be over eighteen.'

I slapped my forehead. 'Idiot, Elizabeth! Of course it's a special, isn't it? Junior riders only. Aren't any of the boys here up to it?'

'Unfortunately not.' Colin came into the kitchen, and although the tired grooves around his mouth looked deeper, he still had a determined air about him. 'There's only one other under-eighteen at Tanglewood who stands any chance of beating that young devil.'

Darren stared at him. 'You can't, Dad! She's never ridden a big course like that and Tosh is so strong when he's galloping out doors. He'll run away with her.'

'With who?' I said ungrammatically. 'Who d'you mean? Wendy – no, she's nineteen, I know.'

(I told you I'm slow sometimes.)

'But you're only sixteen, Liz,' Colin said gently. 'And you're a very good rider indeed.'

He'd never, ever said that before. And I'm actually not quite sixteen yet.

I felt as if someone had squeezed me so hard all my breath had vanished.

'Me!' I squeaked.

Darren had gone quite pale again. 'No, you mustn't. You *are* good, but he's too strong.'

'It's your decision, of course, Liz.' Colin was watching me closely. 'And if you don't want to do it...'

'*Course* I want to do it.' I was up and dancing around, breathing fully restored. 'And I won't let you down. We're going to win, me and Toshak. We're going to beat that vicious Ian Daccombe and rub his oily face in the dirt. We're going to win!'

TEN

THERE WAS QUITE a racket in the kitchen actually, what with me doing a somewhat premature victory song and dance, Darren and Colin arguing, and the dogs joining in for good measure.

'Let's have some hush.' Colin held up his hands and the dogs and I stopped immediately. Darren did a bit more muttering and slammed his cup down a few times, but eventually silence reigned. 'Leave it like this,' Colin suggested. 'We've all had one hell of a day and need a bit of peace and quiet to get over it. I'll go out with Liz tomorrow and watch her take Toshak round your jumping course on the moor. I'll see how you get on, Liz, and *you* see how you feel about the next day's competition. We won't make any firm decisions till then.'

'But...' Darren's face was still tense.

'I agree,' I said quickly. 'And if I *can* manage him OK, you'll feel all right about me doing the cross-country, won't you, Darren?'

'I just don't want you – either of you – hurt,' he muttered. 'I can't stand Ian getting away with all this *and* winning the competition either, but...'

'That's settled then.' Colin got up briskly. 'I've still got a million things to do, including finding the ornament my Uncle gave me. Remember that?'

'Phew, the bloomin' dark horse,' I said. 'I'll stay and help you look if you want.'

'I want you to go home and have a nice early night.' Colin steered me towards the door. 'You've got a couple of really big days ahead so forget Tanglewood and all its torments for a while. I'll sling your bike in the back of the Land Rover and give you a lift.'

He swung off down the path and I turned to look at

Darren. 'Are you OK?'

He smiled with an effort. 'Sure. The arm doesn't hurt now it's in plaster, just a bit achy and heavy. Liz...'

'Mmm?' I hesitated at the door.

'Don't do this Toshak thing if you're not sure.'

I grinned at him with more confidence than I felt. 'I told you – it'll be a doddle. See you in the morning.'

Colin was very talkative all the way home, though I felt slightly out of it and dreamlike. There was too much going on in my brain. As Sasha is keen to point out, it's not the best brain in the world and it was feeling the strain.

'Bill took the news about the money and Uncle Edward and so on very well,' Colin said as we turned the corner into my road. 'I thought he'd class me all sorts of a fool for getting into such a mess but he was surprisingly understanding.'

'Of course he was,' I tried to stifle a yawn. 'It's only *you* who thinks you were an idiot.'

'Beautifully put.' Colin got out and lifted my bike down. 'You have such a way with words sometimes. Get a good night's sleep, Liz. And – thanks.'

I wasn't sure what he was thanking me for but I was suddenly so tired I didn't care. I munched my way automatically through my supper, had a quick bath and was in bed and asleep before it was even dark. (I must be getting old.) My dreams were varied and violent and I woke several times with pounding heart and sweaty palms, convinced Toshak and I were being chased by a weasel wielding wire-cutters. (Try saying that with your mouth full.)

I crawled out of bed at six and hurtled straight off to Tanglewood again. (I do spend time with my own family sometimes, honestly!)

Either the dreams had really got to me, or I was more

worried than I dared admit about Toshak's safety, but I couldn't wait to grab his feed and run to his stable, hoping he'd still be lying down so I could have a good cuddle. Whoever was doing the 'early shift' of morning feeds wasn't around so I did exactly that – grabbed his bowl and scurried across the yard to his box.

I just cannot describe the sinking, aching, jolting shock when I slid back the bolt and stepped into a horribly silent and completely empty stable. I put the bucket on the floor and tried to stem my rising flood of panic. Someone had already turned him out, I reasoned, that was it, an early start and they'd put Tosh in one of the paddocks. But they wouldn't, he's working today and anyway I've got his morning feed, I argued with myself.

'Liz?' I spun round to see Wendy looking over the door at me.

'You're as white as a sheet,' she said 'What's the – oh heck, you went in there to feed Tosh, didn't you?'

I nodded dumbly.

'It's all right. Don't look like that. *It's all right.*'

'Where is he?' I managed to croak.

'He's in the end stable, nearest the house. The Governor wired the door up with an alarm that would ring in the house if anyone touched it.'

So it wasn't just me who'd been worrying about Toshak's safety.

'Nothing happened, though?' I asked her anxiously.

She shook her head. 'No. Tosh is fine. I looked in on him as soon as I got here, and he was still snoring.' She paused and rubbed the back of her neck in an embarrassed way. 'Liz, I'm...I'm so sorry I told Ian Daccombe where the horse would be yesterday.'

'You weren't to know what a terrible thing he'd do,' I said, trying not to feel angry with her.

'No, of course not, and anyway we don't actually *know*

it was him who cut the fence, do we?' She looked at me pleadingly. 'I mean, it might be just a coincidence. Ian would hardly have asked directions from someone who knew him, would he?'

'He's arrogant enough for anything,' I said bluntly. 'Ian Daccombe is so spoilt he thinks he's got a charmed life. He knew all he had to do was deny everything and his doting daddy would believe him.'

'You don't think it could have been someone else then?' Wendy's voice was wistful. 'I honestly didn't see him when I went over to Beech. There was no sign of anyone.'

'He didn't hang about, that's for sure.' I hesitated, wondering whether it would be tactful to ask her *why* she'd gone to the field. 'Um...Ian told you he wanted to take Toshak's photo, didn't he? I don't suppose you noticed if he had a camera?'

'No, but there was a pannier on the back of his bike. It could have been in there. I...I went across to see if he needed help getting Tosh to pose or whatever.'

'I see,' I said, and was careful not to look at her eager, rather plain face. 'Well, I don't suppose we'll ever get any proof if it was Ian and his photographic wire-cutters, so we'll just have to make sure we always keep Tosh safe, won't we? I'm off to give the lad his breakfast, see ya later.'

Tosh was awake, but still lying down when I reached the end box. I couldn't wait to get inside and give him the biggest hug yet. I still hadn't fully recovered from the awful moment I'd stepped into his own, empty stable. I was telling him all about it when two, identically worried faces appeared at the door.

'Liz!' Colin smiled with relief. 'Early as ever. You set the alarm off and frightened us to death. You're supposed to unhook it, didn't Wendy tell you?'

'Sorry.' I got to my feet and Toshak scrambled up too,

pushing his nose eagerly into Darren's outstretched hand.

'Hi-ya, mate,' Darren said to him and looked straight at me. 'You OK?'

'We're both fine.' I tipped Tosh's feed into the manger and came out of the stable. 'So. No break-ins *or* break-outs through the night, that's good. Any luck with the bronze ornament?'

'Not so far, I'm afraid. Come on up and have some breakfast,' Colin invited me. 'Wendy wants to do all the chores on her own. I think she's having a bad time feeling guilty about yesterday.'

'I will then,' I said. 'Thanks.'

We sat down to a huge breakfast, cooked and served up by the Governor himself. 'You're a good cook, Colin,' I said in surprise. I'd only ever had the occasional sandwich at Tanglewood before.

'We both are.' He grinned at his son. 'We've had enough practice over the years. When Darren was little we had a full-time housekeeper but now we've got Annie who just comes in three or four times a week to help with the housework and shopping.'

'I like it better this way.' Darren was struggling one-handedly. 'Dad does much better grub than our housekeeper used to...*Now* what's the matter?'

Colin was staring at us goggle-eyed and open-mouthed. He looked like a handsome goldfish with grey hair. 'You're going to think I'm senile.' He gulped and pushed his plate away. 'I can't seem to think of anything unless you trigger me off, Liz. The ornament, the bronze horse, I've remembered where it is.'

'Terrific! So what's the problem?' Darren had abandoned trying to tackle his breakfast with a fork and was shovelling everything on his plate into an enormous toast sandwich.

'I gave it away.' His father gave him a look of such apologetic despair it was almost comical.

'You...' Darren stopped in mid-bite.

'Who to?' I screamed. (I think that should have been 'to whom' but don't tell me.)

'Mrs Jenkins. The housekeeper. I hadn't thought about her for years, but talking about it to you, Liz, I've just remembered. She admired the bronze and I wasn't too fussed about it, so I gave it her one day. I just gave it her!'

'OK, don't panic.' Darren stood up and waved the sandwich slightly wildly. 'Mrs Jenkins retired and went to live with her mother or someone in Eastbourne or somewhere.'

'You're right, only it was a sister in Hastings.' Colin's worried look was back with a vengeance.

'And you still send her Christmas cards, don't you?' Darren carried on blithely. 'So there we are, we have her address, we know where our dark horse is, there *is* no problem.'

'Your ethics, or lack of them, worry me sometimes.' Colin was pacing round the room like a caged tiger. 'I *gave* the horse to Mrs Jenkins. Didn't lend it or say I'd have it back if it turned out to be valuable. Now you think I should just phone her up and say I didn't mean to give it away so can I have it back? Life's not like that.'

'Not for us anyway.' Darren was really steamed up. 'Ethics are one thing, but throwing away our only chance of keeping Tanglewood is nothing short of crazy.'

'Hoy, simmer down you two!' I felt like a very small referee in a ring with two very large boxers. Not the dogs, the fighters. 'Before you start falling out over the rights and wrongs of your Mrs Jenkins and this bronze horse, we don't even know if it *is* the answer to Uncle Edward's riddle.'

Colin took a deep breath and tried to control his

temper. 'True.'

'So what *is* the answer?' Darren was full of pent-up frustration.

'I don't know,' I admitted. 'But we will find out. Let's get this cross-country competition out of the way and settle Ian Daccombe's hash first. Then we can really concentrate on finding the *dark horse of your own.*'

Both their faces were set in mulish expressions. I think the world of these two, but I'd be the first to admit they're stubborn. Colin and I set off for the yard to get the riding school's day reorganised to allow time for him to accompany me and Tosh across the moor. Darren stayed in the house. He said his arm was hurting and I think he was still sulking a bit.

I hung back and hissed at him, 'What are you going to do?'

'Phone our old housekeeper, of course,' he kicked a chair moodily. 'Honesty's one thing but giving up a possible fortune's something else. Mrs Jenkins wouldn't want to keep a priceless antique anyway. She only liked the horse because it was pretty, I bet.'

'Your dad will go mad if you ask for it back,' I warned him.

'I won't. I'll explain the position and see if she'll agree to have it valued. It's then up to her if it turns out to be worth a fortune. She was a nice old thing, plenty of *ethics* of her own. She'll want Dad to have it.'

'It's all getting too complicated for me,' I complained. 'I can't think further than tomorrow. Wish me luck out on the moor.'

'I do.' He looked at me, his dark eyes sombre. 'Please be careful, Liz. I...couldn't bear you to be hurt. Getting back at Ian Daccombe's just not worth the risk.'

'I won't get hurt. And it's more than getting back at him, it's the pride of Tanglewood at stake!'

86

The silly phrase brought a reluctant grin to his face. 'Get you, duckie,' he said.

I blew him a theatrical kiss and went off to get Tosh ready. To say I was nervous is a slight understatement. I loved the horse dearly, and thoroughly enjoyed schooling him in the manège or jumping in the confined space of the sand school, but he was a different proposition out in the wide open spaces. And if I couldn't control him today there was no way Colin was going to let me take him in the cross-country. I hadn't realised just how much I wanted to get back at Ian, but now there was a chance of doing just that I wanted to go for it with an all-consuming passion.

I knew Ian was the one who'd cut that fence, and it wasn't just the thought of what might have been if our horses had reached the main road that was firing my anger against him. It was the reality of Darren in pain, pain caused directly by Ian Daccombe's vicious actions. My fists clenched involuntarily and I had to make myself relax before going into Toshak's new stable.

Just being with him calmed me, and after I'd brushed him till he shone, tidied his mane and tail and picked out his feet, I was feeling much better. Poor old Darren, I thought, no wonder he's blowing his top this morning. He must be feeling so frustrated at not being able to compete, he and Tosh love it so much.

Colin stuck his head in to see how I was doing. 'There are a couple of private lessons I have to take before we can get going,' he said. 'OK to get this monster warmed up and ready to leave in an hour or so?'

'OK with me, Governor.' I pretended to touch my cap to him, only I wasn't wearing one. It was nice to see him smile. The tension was building up in him too, what with worrying about the huge worries of Tanglewood, the hidden fortune, Darren's injury and the threat to Toshak. All the stuff I was worrying about actually – only more so. He and Darren hated falling out with each other too, although they'd been doing it fairly often recently.

I sighed and wished fervently into Tosh's silky mane that everything would work out and we'd all live happily ever after. Unfortunately, this not being a fairy story, there wasn't a blinding flash and a pumpkin or whatever, just the stark reality of a big, fit, super-keen horse, a frighteningly big jumping course to go round and *me* to ride it. I gulped a few times, gave the horse a final polish and went to get his tack.

Wendy was in the tack room, giving a saddle a thorough going over. She hadn't stopped all morning, patently doing her best to make amends for yesterday's fiasco. I lifted down Tosh's stuff and she said, still a bit shyly, 'Good luck. Hope he goes well for you today.'

'Thanks, Wendy. I hope so too. I really do want to enter the cross-country tomorrow.'

'I want you to, as well.' The words tumbled out. 'I know you can beat Ian Daccombe. His horse is good, but nowhere near as fast as Toshak.'

'You won't tell him, will you?' I was startled into saying. 'We want him to think Tosh will be withdrawn.'

She looked hurt. 'No, I won't tell him. He...he doesn't usually bother to speak to me when I see him anyway. Only when he wants to know something.'

'Sorry.' I felt ashamed. 'I wasn't getting at you. You've given up on the idea that someone else might have let the horses out then?'

'Oh, yes,' she sighed. 'I talked to Bill and, like you, he said it's so obvious. I just wish now I'd got there quicker and actually caught Ian in the act. He'll never own up to it, you know.'

'Let's forget it then,' I said, more cheerfully than I felt. 'We're going to beat him tomorrow *and* I'm going to let

88

him know we're just waiting for him to try his tricks on us again.'

'You can tell him I'll murder him for one, if he ever shows his face round here.' She sounded so fierce I didn't fancy Ian Daccombe's chances at chatting her up again.

I took my tack and marched back to the stable. Right, my darlin' dark horse, I thought. Here we go!

ELEVEN

I DON'T THINK I've ever worked so hard in my life. Toshak was full of beans, having been kept in for much longer than usual. The warm-up did not go brilliantly: he danced when he should have stood, jogged when he should have walked and bucketed when he should have basculed. I persevered until my arms and legs felt like cooked spaghetti. And I still had to go out on the moor yet!

Colin rode over to the sand school on Talisman, his beautiful chestnut warmblood. 'You two look like a circus act at the moment,' he commented and my heart sank.

'He's just over-excited, not having been turned out.' I made excuses. 'I'll settle him down once we're out.'

I did my best to make the bay horse walk properly and we managed the lane in a reasonable fashion. As soon as we reached the moor, though, it was all hell let loose as he plunged and snorted, cavorting just the way he used to when he first arrived at Tanglewood.

'You'd think he'd never been schooled in his life.' Colin was frankly disapproving. 'If you can't manage him, Liz, let me ride him. I'll...'

'No.' I ungritted my teeth, and made myself relax and soften.

You shouldn't ever enter a fight with a horse – they're so much stronger, they're bound to win – and Tosh in particular just won't listen if you start to battle. I kept my hands light, giving small half checks to keep the contact, and thankfully he dropped his nose, came onto the bit and stepped out like an angel.

'There!' I said (or rather panted). 'That's better.'

Colin gave us a searching, appreciative look. 'Are you still going to do this Grand National course you've built?'

'It's hardly that,' I said, thanking my stars it wasn't. 'But, as Darren says, one of the jumps is a lot bigger than anything I've ever attempted. We know Tosh can do it, so let's find out if the same goes for me.'

'You're a game girl.' Colin chuckled and moved Talisman smoothly into canter. 'But I don't want you doing this competition tomorrow if you're not absolutely happy about it. My son is quite right about that – beating Ian Daccombe would be wonderful, but it's not imperative. We all badly want to get back at him in some way, though I really should be spending the time following up this clue of my uncle's. I seem to be making a total hash of everything connected with it, don't I?'

'It'll work out,' I said. 'And we *need* to win tomorrow to show Ian he can't go through life steam-rollering anyone who gets in his way.'

'True. I'd like to do a little flattening of that young man myself.' The glint in his eye said it all.

Whatever the outcome of the cross-country, I didn't think Ian was going to enjoy his day too much, with the entire Tanglewood team breathing fire at him.

We were now approaching the jumps, cantering uphill to the stone wall, which Tosh popped over, barely bothering to glance at it, then across two wide and uneven ditches, which he gauged perfectly, and on down a steepish slope leading to the stream. The big bay horse was thoroughly enjoying himself and starting to pull eagerly. I stayed calm and found I could hold him, riding positively between the jumps and reading our take-off positions properly.

Colin was following us. I could hear the steady pounding of Talisman's hooves, but didn't let Tosh turn the course into a race, just kept him at a fast but steady pace, and concentrated on each jump as it came. We'd almost done the full circle and only had the log piles now.

91

I felt a small thrill of fear when I saw that the big one we'd built up for Darren was still intact.

I'm not kidding, it looked *huge* as we approached it. But I didn't rush, just maintained plenty of impulsion, judged the take-off – and we simply *flew* over it. We surged on to a final smaller jump, landing in the stream, leaping up the bank and onto the turf the other side, still cantering smoothly. Perfect, it had been perfect. I gradually slowed down and brought Tosh to a halt. He was sweating only lightly and his heartbeat rate was hardly raised. A very fit young man, our Tosh.

Colin and Talisman joined us, grinning. (Colin mostly.) 'Well *done*, Liz. The big jump was quite formidable, wasn't it? Talis and I didn't do it with anything like such style.' He patted his horse's neck and looked at me, dark eyes serious now. 'So, what do you think about tomorrow?'

'No question,' I said unhesitatingly. 'Tosh does pull, but it's nothing I can't handle. Once I've got him concentrating he's wonderful. Push the button and away he goes.'

'Yes, dead easy, isn't it?' Colin winked at me. 'Don't you put yourself down, Elizabeth. You rode that beautifully. The thing you have to remember is that you two have just cleared a dozen or so familiar obstacles on familiar ground. Tomorrow's cross-country is unknown territory: there are thirty very varied fences and a lot of galloping between them.'

THIRTY! I nearly passed out. 'No problem,' I said, as airily as I could. 'Toshak's as fit as a flea and he's very bold. I don't think the unknown will worry him.' It might frighten the life out of me, I thought.

We were walking steadily towards home, though Tosh kept looking hopefully towards the gallop track. 'Look at him!' I laughed. 'He's really keen for more.'

'And you?' Colin was still looking searchingly at me.

'Yes, me too. I can't wait for tomorrow,' I said firmly, pushing away the thought of all those fences.

'OK.' Colin seemed to relax at last. 'We'll do it then. You and Toshak will enter the competition, but you're to know that you don't have to pull out all the stops to beat Ian. You're totally inexperienced in this kind of class and we'll all be thrilled if you just get round.'

'Pooh, get round nuthin'.' I made a face at him. 'I told you we're going to win, aren't we, Tosh?'

'Just don't go mad, that's all.' Colin prodded me gently with his stick. 'You and Toshak are to have the rest of the day off – No!' He stemmed my flow of protest. 'Tosh will be better for letting off some of that steam in one of the fields, and you still look tired. Flop about and catch up on some sleep. That's an order.'

'You won't put him back in Beech, will you?' I said worriedly.

'No. None of them are going back in there till we've made it more secure.' Colin smiled reassuringly. 'Toshak will be in one of the paddocks next to the yard and will be checked every five minutes. That good enough?'

'Yep. But if I'm not going to be working I could spend some more time looking for the dark horse clue. We've got to find it.'

'Oh, I know we have.' We were nearing Tanglewood's gate and the worried frown had reappeared on Colin's face. 'That money's got to show up soon, but you've done enough all round, Liz. Leave it to us for now, and stop worrying.'

To be honest, the thought of a lazy day seemed quite amazingly appealing, so for once I did as I was told. Darren had gone back to hospital for some readjustment to his plaster, so after watching Tosh's ecstatic roll in the dirtiest bit of field he could find, I went home. My mum was surprised to see me, but as usual was very helpful about sorting out the stuff I was to wear the next day and organising some nice food to take with me.

I had a really long, wallowy bath with chocolate-scented essence. It's brilliant. You come out all soft and silky and you smell like a Jaffa cake. I washed my hair as well and considered moussing and gelling and blow-drying, but decided I had enough to cope with the next day without rampant hair, and let it dry sleek and natural. I was going to do, unusually for me, a couch-potato act and watch all the afternoon soaps on TV but Sasha dropped by on the way home from school, so we went up to my room for a gossip instead.

'So what's new?' She took up her usual position by the dressing table. Her hair was in a French plait, very chic and sophisticated. Mine was in a pigtail down my back. Very twelve years old.

'I don't know where to begin,' I said, and leapt straight in with the finding of the clue, the dark horse hunt, Colin's reaction, the Daccombes, the runaway horses, Darren's broken arm and my unexpected entry into the world of cross-country competition.

'Blimey.' She stared at me with respect. 'I always thought you led a boring life but how wrong can I be? I *was* right about the secret drawer, though? Fancy that!'

'I was going to phone and tell you yesterday,' I said guiltily. 'But I fell asleep.'

'S'okay.' she shrugged. 'It was a real long shot, and Darren was the one who found it, not me. Tell me again what was on the piece of paper.'

I recited Uncle Edward's riddle. Tennyson it wasn't but I knew it off by heart. Sasha's analytical brain was at work straightaway.

'You were following completely the wrong line searching the stable,' she said. 'It just doesn't fit the clue.'

'We know that now but at the time it seemed logical.' I

was nettled. She can be so superior.

'I really need to see the desk and its contents.' She was deeply into the solving of the mystery, I could see that, but my heart still sank at the thought of taking her to Tanglewood.

'I'd show it to you,' I said weakly, 'but I don't think Colin and Darren want anyone else poking and prying around the place.'

'It sounds as though they could do with all the help they can get,' Sasha said, rather snappily I thought. 'You're all just going round in circles, getting nowhere fast, and falling out with each other in the process.'

'No, we're not. Colin and Darren have had a couple of disagreements, but that's understandable with all the pressure they're under. Neither of them has rowed with me, in fact Darren's...' I stopped.

'Getting keener and keener on you!' Sasha finished triumphantly.

'Don't talk wet.' I was blushing.

'And you...don't be coy. He couldn't make it more obvious – getting in a jealous rage when Ian Daccombe chatted you up, holding your hand, wanting that black horse to win, but not wanting *you* to take the risk of riding him...'

'Whoa, hang on.' She takes my breath away sometimes. 'I don't remember telling it quite like that, Sasha.'

'You didn't.' She pulled my plait gently. 'But I know what's what. Darren showed all the classic signs of the jealous male when he saw you with Ian.'

'Ian has got the face of a weasel and the soul of a rat,' I said. 'Why should anyone, let alone Darren, be bothered by someone like that?'

'Actually Ian's not bad-looking.' Sasha looked at her reflection reflectively. (If that's possible.) 'And he's loaded, absolutely loaded. His dad's got a brand new sports car all lined up for when he passes his test.'

'How do you know that?'

'He told me,' she said calmly. 'He failed the first one, the day after his seventeenth birthday, but he says he's bound to pass it next time.'

'You talk to him!' I said in horror. 'I didn't know that. You haven't been out with him surely?'

'No.' She laughed at my outraged face. 'He's asked me but I just pretend I'm going steady. You never know, though, when he gets his car I just might.'

'Sasha!' I was deeply shocked. It was bad enough that Wendy had liked the thought of being chatted up by Ian. 'You couldn't possibly...'

'Oh, all right. I'm just winding you up. You make him sound like a mass murderer the way you describe him. I know he is a total creep, and getting worse by the sound of it. I was just making the point that Darren cares enough about you to get mad when he thinks another bloke fancies you.'

'Rubbish.' I felt a great glow all the same. 'Darren's just...fond of me, thinks of me as a sister probably.'

'Yeah, yeah.' Sasha did an enormous fake yawn. 'Hold hands with your brother all the time do you, Liz?'

I blushed again and changed the subject before it got too heavy. 'Give it a rest, you. I've got too much on my plate to think about it anyway. I get a real case of the collywobbles every time I think about this competition tomorrow.'

'Why?' Sasha's got no imagination when it comes to horses. 'I thought everything went well today. You found the horse easier to handle out of doors than you thought, didn't you?'

'Sure, but as Colin said, tomorrow's course is a far cry from our circuit on the moor. I don't want to just get round, I want to win. We've got to beat that swine Ian.'

'I think I like "weasel-faced rat" better.' Sasha was trying to lighten my warrior-like mood. 'It's no good worrying. You're such a determined little thing you'll probably do it. Tell you what, greater love has no best friend – I'll come and cheer you on in the morning.'

'What about school?' It was terrible, the way I tried to keep her away from anything to do with Tanglewood. Away from Darren, if I'm honest. If she was right and he was beginning to look at me in a more romantic way, the last thing I wanted was a prettier, cleverer, wittier, *blonder* girl around to distract him.

'No problem' she answered. 'My first two lessons are double study periods. I don't have to be in till lunch-time and you'll probably be round and back by ten o'clock.'

Round and back. She made it sound like a funfair ride.

'Mmm,' I said. 'Will you bring Steve along?'

'Nah.' She started undoing her hair. 'I finished with him yesterday. I'm going to go for men with brains in future. Good looks are OK but you get so *bored*, don't you?'

'Chance would be a fine thing,' I said lightly, trying to imagine being bored with Darren. 'So my debut into the world of cross-country is to be made doubly auspicious by the presence of Miss Sasha Beaumont. Aren't I the lucky one!'

She fluffed out her hair and looked at her devastatingly pretty face in the mirror. 'You sure are. And if you're good I'll also solve your bloomin' dark horse mystery while I'm there.'

In my dreams that night, as well as wire-cutting weasels looking amazingly like Ian Daccombe, I had willowy blonde filmstars draping themselves lovingly over my handsome, dark-eyed hero. He had one arm in a sling and I was galloping on a dark bay horse with wings, trying to catch up with him.

Just as we approached a jump built like the Eiffel Tower, the weasel cut off the top of it with his wire-cutters, the one-armed hero kissed the blonde filmstar, the dark horse spread his wings and flew off, and I fell thankfully into a deep, quiet pool of sleep.

TWELVE

I SUPPOSE I was lucky to get *any* sleep with so much going on in my head, but sleep I did, and woke up feeling confused but raring to go. Colin was picking me up in the horsebox (real star treatment), which meant I didn't have such an early start as usual and could talk to my parents at breakfast. They were both thrilled for me, getting the chance to enter such a prestigious competition, though my mum, as ever, was worrying.

'It's such short notice. I'd have got the morning off to watch you if we'd known earlier.' She works part-time in a doctors' surgery. 'And so would your dad.'

'I know you would.' I gave them both a hug. 'Tell you what, I'll ask Colin to take a video. He won't be able to record the whole course, but hopefully you'll see my moment of glory.'

They both came out to wave me off when the horsebox arrived. My mum was calling out, 'Good luck! Take care... don't fall off,' and other embarrassing motherly things, and then we turned the corner and were off.

'Nervous?' Darren looked at me, the new warmth very apparent in his eyes.

I dropped my own eyes, quite shyly. 'A bit. How's Tosh?'

'He's great. Never looked fitter. I hear he behaved beautifully for you yesterday. How did you manage that? I've been taking him over the moor for years and he still pulls like a train with me.'

'Some horses do go more kindly for a woman rider,' Colin said.

Woman, not girl – what progress!

'I just hope he remembers that today then,' I said fervently. 'Will you go through the course with me as soon as we arrive? I need to know the worst.'

'Surely,' Colin said, keeping his eyes on the road, but making a little bow. 'We are your grooms and your servants this morning, ma'am. I've given us both the day off from the school – we're going to watch you put young Daccombe firmly in his place, then spend the rest of the day tracking down Uncle Edward's riddle.'

I raised my eyebrows and looked at Darren. He read it correctly as 'Did you phone the housekeeper?' He shook his head and mouthed 'No reply' silently.

'What are you two whispering about?' Colin demanded. He seemed to have recovered his high spirits and optimism today, and I was glad to see that he and his son were back on good terms. They just couldn't stay bad friends for long.

'We were discussing Einstein's theory of relativity,' Darren replied solemnly.

'Get away,' Colin said, grinning. 'What's that then, how to put up with your relatives? We're here, people!'

We pulled into the competitors' parking area at the manor house which was hosting the competition. Its grounds were huge and beautifully landscaped and I couldn't wait to see the spectacular course they'd had built. I didn't have to wait long. We reported to the secretary, got my number – *thirteen*, would you believe? – my starting time, 9.20, and the course plan. I nearly died, and who wouldn't?

1. Rails and gorse hedge – 2. Log pile – 3. Tree trunk – 4. Hayrack – 5. Sloping rails – 6. Stone wall – 7. Bullfinch – 8. Corner (bounce) rails – 9. Hedge and oxer – 10. River crossing – 11. Rails out of river – 12. Bank out of road – 13. Trakehner – 14. Steps down – 15. Double bounce – 16. Hedge and ditch – 17. Cage (circle) – 18. Rails into road – out of road – 19. Hedge and drop – 20. Normandy bank – 21. Trout hatchery – 22. Table – 23. Double coffin – 24. Zig-

I rest my case. I rested myself too, sitting down a bit sharply and taking a few deep intakes of breath. Darren had unloaded Tosh, hopped on and was walking him round. The bay horse adored competitions and was always up on his toes immediately he arrived, but I noticed he was doing none of the usual prancing and jigging, seemingly aware of Darren's one-handed touch and of the broken arm in its sling.

'Should you be doing that?' I asked Darren sternly, hoping my shaking knees didn't show.

'I just wish I could take him round the course,' he smiled down at me and my knees seemed to shake even more. 'It looks a beauty, doesn't it?'

Not quite my idea of beauty, but still. Colin and I left him with the horse and went off to do a thorough inspection. I will only say that the jumps looked worse than they sounded.

When the young riders began to set off, each one seemed to have trouble with a different fence, the corner rails catching the first rider, who also refused the river crossing. The steps down and downhill rails caught a couple more off guard, and the Normandy bank caused the downfall, literally, of another. Before I knew it, it was time for me to pop Tosh over the practice fence and get myself to the start. As soon as he felt a two-armed rider aboard, the wicked horse did a quick personality change and started sweating up and dancing.

'He'll soon settle when he sees what's expected of him,' Colin said, a trifle grimly I thought. 'You won't have time to rock 'n' roll on this course, Toshak.'

Darren squeezed my calf and I looked down into his anxious face.

'We'll be fine,' I said, in a voice that didn't sound as if it belonged to me.

His concerned eyes were fixed on my face, and then we were off, galloping the long, slightly uphill stretch to the gorse and rails. We were going too fast I knew, but I couldn't bring the big horse back. There wasn't a lot of judgment on my part with the first three jumps, but luckily they were straightforward and Tosh's natural ability got him safely over.

He gave the hayrack a hefty clout and that seemed to sober him up. I could feel him listening and responding at last. My own nerves had gone; I was too busy and exhilarated to shake any more. I wondered briefly about the corner rails – I'd never done any before – but we did the manoeuvre perfectly. The river crossing, of course, presented no problem to our water-loving boy, and the next few obstacles, though unfamiliar to me, were beautifully built and positioned and we cleared them all.

We were more than half way round, and though my arms were feeling a little stretched, they were holding out. Tosh's speed was well in excess of the pace I'd been told to set. Colin was perched up on a hill videoing us, I knew, but it was Darren who'd be doing most of the worrying. We took the bank all wrong, slipped, slithered, and nearly fell, but somehow I stayed on board and somehow this wonderful, clever horse stayed on his feet. Slightly shaken if not stirred we treated the next jumps with more respect. The zig-zag rails confused Tosh a little, but I remembered my instructions, held him together and we nipped safely, if slightly raggedly, through. I was starting to feel tired. I'd never ridden this hard this far before, but Toshak was in his element.

He took the quarry and the wagon literally in his stride, but was impeded by me getting my weight too far forward at the downhill rails. You could almost hear the horse give a patient sigh as I lumped inelegantly around but it didn't really slow him, and he soared the next two fences as if we'd only just started. One to go, I couldn't believe it. For a moment, panic struck me and I imagined us ducking out or falling, or both. Tosh merely said, 'Arrowhead, goodeee' and whizzed away. A slightly undulating two-hundred yard run-in to the finish – and that was it! Easy as pie!

I yelled aloud – a great mixture of delight, relief and incredulity. Darren was running to greet us, his face alight with excitement and something else I couldn't read. He caught hold of the bridle with his good hand and I leapt down and threw my arms around him. I could hear the strong pounding of his heart and feel the weight of the plaster as he tried to encircle me awkwardly with his broken arm.

'I'm hurting you,' I said, and looked up to see that same, fathomless expression on his face.

'No, you're not,' he smiled, and kissed the very tip of my nose. 'That's for being a winner. And you are.'

I knew he wasn't talking about the competition. Colin appeared at a smart jog, video camera in hand.

'Brilliant. Brilliant. Absolutely brilliant!' He was dancing. 'You should see Ian Daccombe's face!'

'He saw Tosh do it then?' I asked eagerly.

'He saw you *both* do it.' Colin patted my back exuberantly. 'You frightened me to death a couple of times, Liz, but you were superb. You were both superb. The Daccombes are green. Ian goes off in a few minutes, but there's no way he can beat your time.'

'Which was a lot faster than I told you to go,' Darren said in mock severity.

We were walking back to the horsebox to get Toshak's antisweat rug so we could walk him round to get him cooled down. As we approached I could see a slim figure leaning against the cab. I'd told Darren and his dad

Sasha might come over to watch, but I'd been secretly hoping she wouldn't. Darren had been non-committal, but I couldn't forget his comment about her good looks, and if he found out she was bright as well...it didn't bear thinking about.

I hoped she'd be unsuitably dressed, teetering about on high heels or wearing something embarrassing in Lycra, but no, she looked great. Her hair was in the flattering French plait again and she was wearing well-cut corduroy trousers, a fabulous dark sweater and *green wellies*. (She must have borrowed them specially, I really couldn't see Sasha including them in her usual wardrobe.)

'You missed it.' I greeted her rather curtly I suppose. Well, if she's there to cheer me on, the least she could do was turn up on time.

'No, I saw the whole thing, except when you disappeared in a cloud of spray into the river.' She nodded hello to Darren. 'You did quite well, didn't you, Liz?'

'You could say that.' Colin looked amused, but Darren, to my shameful delight, was glaring at her in irritation.

'Liz was incredible,' he said.

'Well done, mate.' Sasha is incorrigible, never one to be put down. 'And what about Ian 'The Ripper' Daccombe?'

'Shush.' I couldn't help giggling. 'One of his friends might hear.'

'He has *friends*?' She feigned amazement. 'I thought from what you said no human being or even alien lifeforce could tolerate the air he breathes.'

Colin laughed aloud. 'Liz sees everything and everyone in shades of black or white. And that young man committed the heinous crime of cruelty to horses, bad enough on its own, but his last attempt was directed at this chap here.'

'Ah, the famous *dark horse*.' Sasha touched his sweaty

neck cautiously.

I felt Colin stiffen and silently cursed my best friend for letting him realise, with that one expression, that she'd been told all about our mystery.

I couldn't look directly at Colin, just fiddled around with the sweat rug and said over-casually, 'Sasha said she'd help with the riddle solving. She's good. It was her idea that there'd be a secret drawer.'

'So you said.' I thought Colin had taken to her, but the warmth had gone out of his voice. 'Just how much do you know about Tanglewood's affairs, Miss Beaumont?'

'Affairs?' Sasha clowned. 'I thought you'd all be far too busy looking for the real dark horse to have affairs. You are awful!'

For a moment I thought Colin was going to blow his top, but his sense of humour won through and he reluctantly grinned at her.

'Oh, well, I suppose I deserve to be made fun of. A laughing stock is what I've made of myself and I guess little Liz needed to talk to someone with a bit of sense. She's more or less held us two idiots together these last few days.'

'That's Liz's speciality.' Sasha smiled at me. 'She gives me a hard time when I'm being unbearable, you know, my usual cocky self, but she's the greatest friend in the world when I need her.'

Honestly, how embarrassing. All this praise on top of a great cross-country debut was too much for me.

'I'm glad I'm in favour,' I said. 'But if you don't mind I'll leave you now. I want to walk Tosh round to cool him off.'

'I'll come with you,' Darren said immediately and I pretended not to see Sasha doing her lovelorn swoon act.

'OK.' I was really pleased he wanted to be with me and Toshak. We took the horse walkabout, with me getting more and more embarrassed at all the congratulations and good wishes from spectators and competitors alike. Darren spotted an ice-cream van and insisted on going over to buy a double triple-chocolate-layer whopper to celebrate.

I stood leaning happily against the bay's side letting him crop some of the parkland's sweet grass. I supposed the junior competition would soon be over – there were twenty-four entered so it was threequarters of the way through already, and Ian Daccombe would have done his round.

'Don't pretend you didn't watch.' The furious voice could have been reading my mind and I looked up sharply.

'No pretence, I didn't.' I said bluntly. 'I have no desire to watch you do *anything*, Ian. Except squirm, maybe.'

'Oh, yeah.' He jabbed his sweat-covered horse cruelly in the flanks with his spurs. 'I'd have beaten you, you snotty bitch, if I'd had a decent horse. This cretin messed up the water and wouldn't do the rails. I was faster, I bet.'

'You might have been,' I said coolly. 'Unlike me you wouldn't have considered your horse. But 'might have' doesn't count, does it? I beat you, *we* beat you, Toshak and I and Tanglewood.'

'And I'll get you back, don't worry.' He yanked savagely on the reins and I noticed his hands. Harsh hands certainly, not yielding and considerate, but it was their shape that suddenly caught my attention.

'Forget it,' I said quickly. 'You won't ever come near us again. Your father will see to that. And I wonder if you'll ever get that sports car once we've proved it was you who cut our fences and chased the horses out? Chased them to their probable deaths. Your dad's not going to like that, Ian.'

'Stop bluffing. You can't prove a thing. That pudding of a groom thinks I was there because I fancy her and she

106

didn't *see* anything anyway. Are you saying you were hiding your cute little self behind a bush, now Lizzie?'

'Not my little self no, but there *was* a rather cute security camera in the copse. You saw Colin with the camcorder? He's going to show that earlier clip to your father in a minute.'

'Rubbish.' His face had gone deadly pale. 'If you had my face on film you'd have been round to see Dad with it before now.'

'Not your face, no.' I was plotting desperately. 'But the camera showed, clearly showed, the hand that held those wire-cutters, Ian. It's an unusual hand – and I've just recognised it.'

He clenched his fingers immediately.

'The little finger,' I went on, 'is very elongated. Creepy really, it's almost the same length as the third finger. Extremely rare I should say. D'you think your dad will know whose hand it is?'

He swore again and for a minute I thought he was going to ride his horse straight at me, but, like a one-armed tornado, Darren was between us. He thrust an enormous ice-cream into my hand and grabbed Ian's reins, forcing the horse away with his shoulder. I saw him wince with pain and yelled at him to stop as he made a grab for Ian's arm. Ian snatched, panic-stricken, at the reins and kicked his poor horse viciously again. The startled animal shot nervously forward, and Darren's one-handed grip was loosened. He staggered and nearly fell, watching with impotent rage as Ian ran away from him like a rabbit.

'I'll kill him.' His dark eyes were savage. 'He was going to hurt you, Liz. He was...'

'You stopped him.' I put my hand gently on the broken arm. 'Your poor shoulder, Darren.'

'It's all right.' He took my hand in his good one and

looked into my eyes. 'You're OK? What did he want?'

I told him rapidly about Ian's threat, and the story I'd spun him.

'What's the point in telling him that?' He was perplexed. 'We *don't* have his hand on the video. There was no camera in the wood...'

'But Ian doesn't know that for sure. Let's get back to the horsebox and I'll tell you my scheme.'

We set off, and it wasn't until we were half way there I realised that the amazing cross-country genius, Toshak, had eaten my whopper ice-cream!

THIRTEEN

IT WASN'T REALLY a surprise to find that Darren kept hold of my hand all the way to the horsebox. I saw Sasha and felt suddenly self-conscious, so I pretended to fiddle around with Tosh's bridle in order to release myself without seeming unwelcoming. Sasha's eagle eye had spotted us anyway, I could tell by the knowing grin. I ignored it and her and ran round to see Colin. I told him about our brush with Ian and spelled out my idea about the video. He looked unconvinced at first, and made his usual protest about not telling the truth, but in the end he said we'd give it a try.

'We've nothing to lose I suppose.' He wasn't keen on joining in, the man is totally reluctant to be party to even the most necessary fib.

'And we've got to do *something*,' I said, quite irritably. 'Beating Ian might not have been such a great idea after all. He's now so mad I think he'll have another go at Toshak if we don't stop him.'

'And only his father can really stop him,' Colin agreed. 'OK. I'll go and see him now.'

'You'll have to be quick. Ian's probably on his way.'

I took the camcorder and placed it on the driver's seat of the horsebox in full view of the window. My plan was not a subtle one, but I was banking on Ian being pretty dense as well as desperate. Colin went rapidly over to the Daccombe's big car, parked a short distance away. Darren, Sasha and I hid behind the next door lorry and waited. It seemed hours but I suppose we'd only stood there for five minutes when Colin and a redfaced and reluctant Mr Daccombe joined us.

'This is ridiculous,' the man blustered. 'I do not believe your story for a minute, Mr James. If you had security cameras in operation in the field from where your horses escaped you'd have told me so before.'

'Mr Daccombe, Liz told that story to your son, hoping to provoke a reaction from him. You will agree, won't you, that if Ian had nothing whatsoever to do with the cutting of the fence, he has nothing to fear from any video recording of the event.'

'Of course he's got nothing to be worried about. He didn't do it; he told us both so. You've brought me over here on false pretences and...'

'Ssh!' I hissed urgently.

He turned his angry face towards me. 'What...'

'Be quiet,' I said firmly. 'Look!'

We were all still hidden from view to anyone approaching the Tanglewood horsebox and there was indeed someone sidling rapidly towards it. A hand, a hand with a strangely long little finger, reached out and undid the driver's door. We were all watching when Ian Daccombe picked up the camera, held it above his head, and threw it violently to the ground. He was lifting his heel to stamp and grind it to oblivion when his father gave a strangled cry and ran out from behind the lorry. Ian's pasty face went three shades whiter and his expression of horrified guilt was not a pretty sight.

'Ian! Stop that!' I hadn't realised Mr Daccombe could sound so authoritative.

Ian wilted, his shoulders drooping defeatedly. Given some time he'd probably have thought up a story about wanting to destroy the film of me and Tosh beating him in our cross-country round, but I'd gambled on him crumbling at the sheer shock of his father witnessing his act of destruction. And of course my cunning plan worked!

Ian could do nothing but admit everything and mumble abject apologies to us all. He hung his head and listened to his father tell Colin all the damage his son had

110

caused would be repaid plus a handsome compensation for the mental anguish and physical pain (that was Darren's). Colin pointed out that he could make a court case of Ian's malicious act.

'The shock of that might be good for him in the long run,' he said. 'Ian is in real danger of becoming a major criminal. It's in everyone's interests, including his own, that he is stopped.'

'I know. I do know.' I felt quite sorry for Mr Daccombe, it was as if he was seeing Ian for the first time and hated what was there. 'I've been worried about this aspect of him for some time, but I always convinced myself he wouldn't lie to me. The things he has done are appalling but you have my word, my solemn word, that I still have control of my son, and if you don't call in the police I will guarantee he'll never do you and yours any harm ever again.'

To my relief (my sympathies were entirely with Mr Daccombe Senior, you understand) Colin agreed, and Ian shuffled off miserably in his father's wake.

'Phew!' Sasha said. 'High drama! What about you, old bozobrain Latcham! How on earth did you come up with a plot like that?'

'Because she's clever, that's how.' Darren was protectively at my side again.

'Clever? She's supersonic.' Colin laughed in sheer relief. 'I've said it before and I'll say it again: *what* a girl!'

As if on cue the loudspeaker crackled and announced the conclusion of the juniors riders' competition and listed the scores in reverse order: '...and in first place, twenty-two points ahead, Miss Elizabeth Latcham riding Mr Darren James' Toshak.' I didn't have a huge fan club present, just the three of them, but boy, were they *loud!* They cheered and shouted and clapped and hollered and Darren hugged me again, with his good arm this time.

111

'My moment of glory.' I laughed and looked ruefully at the mud-encrusted camera. 'And I don't have it for posterity to show my mum and dad.'

'The film might be salvaged.' Colin peered hopefully at the thing. 'Get on that horse and collect your cup, wonderwoman, and I'll see if I can get it working to record that, too.'

I was in a real trance after all the excitement so it's lucky he did do just that, or I might have thiught that morning was one of my wilder weird dreams. I collected the prize without having any idea of how to control Tosh, who luckily did the job himself. We did all the booting and bandaging and loading of him and were driving back to Tanglewood before I properly came to.

'I think she's back with us.' Colin grinned at Darren, who squeezed my hand gently.

Sasha was wedged in on my other side, making the front very cosy, to say the least. She was carrying the cup we'd just won and looking as smug as if she'd been round thirty humungous jumps herself.

'I gather you're coming to Tanglewood to do your mystery-solving routine,' I said to her. 'Have you told these two that's what you're doing, or did you just say we were all so fascinating you couldn't bear to leave us?'

'Don't be nasty now. You've had your little triumph, now allow me to have mine.' She showed her teeth in a mock snarl and I, very grown up, crossed my eyes and poked my tongue out at her.

'You two are better than a comedy routine,' Colin said, pulling into the yard.

Wendy came rushing straight over, and there was more squealing and wowing, then I led the cross-country winner to his stable and Bill came in and we went through the whole story again. Darren did most of the talking, while I gently brushed the beautiful bay horse

112

before giving him an extra special feed already prepared by Wendy. She was, if it's possible, as thrilled about the win as me, and possibly even more thrilled about Ian's come-uppance. She said she'd put Tosh out again after he'd rested so Darren and I went up to the house to rejoin Colin and Sasha. They were in the office and we could hear Colin's voice, low and reflective as he reminisced about days long gone.

Darren raised his eyebrows. 'Dad's really taken to your friend. I've never heard him talk like this to anyone.'

'It's probably a reaction to all the pressures and problems,' I said. 'Besides, sometimes it's easier to talk to an outsider.'

'Not for me.' He looked meaningfully at me, the warmth shining in his face.

'So Uncle Edward wasn't a bachelor after all, then?' Sasha's clear voice carried easily into the kitchen and I tried to concentrate on things other than Darren's dark eyes.

'No. He was married as a young man, and, like me, his wife died early in the marriage. I think he sympathised when my wife died, that was the basis of his affection. He felt there was an affinity – an affinity forged by our similar tragedy.'

'And children?' Sasha was being very gentle. 'Did he have children too?'

'In that respect I was much luckier. His wife and their only son died together, in a terrible car crash. The little boy was only two.'

'How awful. No wonder he was so fond of Darren, sending him those Christmas presents and so on.'

'My uncle was fonder of the *idea* of my son than the reality I think,' Colin said. 'After the accident he became totally eccentric and out of touch with the real world. It was me he was fond of, though he spent most of his time

113

making money, contacting us, the only family he had, just occasionally.'

'So who were the riddles for?'

'I can't remember how they came about, but it amused him to write them and I always played along. I wanted the lonely man to be happy. I used to help Darren solve the clues when he was little. I guess the old boy must have thought we were good at them.'

'He was wrong there, wasn't he?' The cheeky element was back in Sasha's voice. I was quite surprised myself at the way she was getting Colin to talk to her. He'd only ever mentioned the illness and death of his wife, Darren's mother, once in all the years I'd known him, and here he was discussing it with a virtual stranger. Sasha's always said she'd like to study to be a psychiatrist, and I wouldn't have been surprised to see Colin lying on a couch with her taking notes, but there I was wrong. In reality it looked even odder.

When we walked in Colin had turned the desk upside down again and was crawling around it, prodding and measuring, and Sasha was sat cross-legged near him, surrounded by sheets of paper and envelopes.

'I thought we'd done all this.' Darren's annoyance was partly caused by his father's seemingly total acceptance of Sasha, I knew. It was uncharacteristic and it worried him. I made a mental note to tell him that, on the other hand, it was totally in character for Sasha.

'Miss Beaumont,' Colin said formally, 'is of the opinion we've been looking at the riddle all wrong.'

His son raised expressive eyebrows. 'Is she now? I didn't know you were an expert, Sasha.'

'Nah – I just use the brains I've got, and unlike you lot, apply them with logic,' she said, quite rudely I thought. She's not used to being talked to as if she's just crawled out of the woodwork, especially not by an attractive male.

114

'Is that right? So where do you think we went astray?' He was actually being sarcastic, but Sasha chose to ignore the fact and answered him seriously.

'The timing. The timing of the clue is all-important. The key words are, I think, *now that you've a dark horse of your own.*'

'Yes, even us thickies agree on that.' Darren was looking at his father who was now tapping the desk all over, placing his ear right on it as he did.

'Yes, but you didn't follow that through logically.' Sash abandoned the letter she was reading and pulled another from its envelope. 'You and Liz promptly rushed off and started searching Toshak, didn't you? I bet you even looked in the fillings in his teeth.'

'Horses don't have...' I began, but caught her eye and stopped in time. 'OK. We finally worked out Tosh isn't the dark horse Uncle Edward meant, but he *was* the most obvious, wasn't he?'

'Not at all.' She shook her blonde head emphatically.

'The bronze horse then? The one Dad gave to Mrs Jenkins?' Darren was becoming more interested in what she was saying.

'I don't think so. The timing's wrong again, you see. Your uncle gave that as a present years ago. And the riddle clearly says *now that you've a dark horse of your own.*'

'*Now,*' I said slowly. 'That's the key word, you think? So it couldn't be Tosh, because he's been here at Tanglewood for several years, too.'

'Clever child,' Sasha said indulgently. (She's three days older. Three days!) 'The dark horse your uncle was referring to was something that arrived at Tanglewood at the *same time* as the riddle itself. *Now* you've a dark horse.'

'So it is the desk?' I'm just not one of the world's clear thinkers.

115

'Definitely not.' Darren was frowning. 'That was our first thought, remember. You think it's something *in* the desk, Sasha?'

'Mmm. Either there's a clue in the contents, or I suppose there could even be a second secret drawer.'

'That's what I'm looking for.' Colin had stopped tapping and was sitting back, looking perplexed. 'Though I'll be blowed if I can see *where* it could be. The one you found is beautifully made and concealed, but there's just no room for another one.'

'Have you tried twisting the other carvings?' Darren went over to join him and I sat down beside Sasha.

'Can I help with this? What are you looking for?'

'No idea.' She was concentrating on deciphering the pointed, old-fashioned writing. 'I'm just reading every word to see if there's a clue hidden in the script.'

'We've all had a go at that,' I said. 'I know you're so much cleverer than us, but they seem like ordinary, genuine letters rather than more riddles. They're so dull for one thing.'

'You're dead right there. I'll keep on with it though. You could try the books, Liz. See if there are any paragraphs or pages marked in some way.'

I picked up the heavy volume on antiques and started ploughing through it. The office was warm and quiet and it felt strange and dreamlike to be sitting there after the high excitement of the morning. We worked steadily for ages, till I felt peckish and went to fetch coffee and biscuits. I carried the tray into the office and handed round mugs. Sasha was reading the last page of the last letter.

She took the coffee, asked for a biscuit and said absent-mindedly 'I don't know why I'm so hungry.'

'Probably because it's nearly lunch-time.' Colin looked at his watch. 'What time do you have to be at school?'

'Oh heck, in ten minutes.' Sasha leapt to her feet. 'I've

116

got to change first too. My mum dropped me off at the Manor this morning and I said I'd ring if I wanted a lift back. Can I use your phone?'

'It'll be quicker if I take you.' Colin picked up his keys. 'We'll carry on looking for the answer this afternoon.'

'I really wanted to find it.' She sounded wistful. 'I'm sure it's here somewhere but I just can't see it. Your uncle truly was a dark horse, wasn't he? Very clever and secretive.'

'Too clever by half.' Darren drank his coffee gloomily and watched her go rushing off. 'He was a bit like your friend in that respect.'

'Sasha *is* clever.' I defended her immediately. 'Don't you like her?'

I think I wanted him to say no but he said, 'She's OK. Better than I thought.'

I wondered miserably if that meant 'better than you, Liz', but he looked at me and suddenly said, 'She's not a patch on you, though, not in looks, personality...nothing. You're...'

It was going too fast for me. I turned away quickly and said somewhat shakily, 'I'm *tidier,* that's what. Look at the mess she's left.'

I sat down and started picking up the sheets of paper left strewn on the floor. Sasha had pulled each letter out, read it, and simply dropped it on the floor. I gathered the letters together and started going through the envelopes, trying to match the dates on the postmarks so I could put each one back correctly.

I was doing all this so I could keep my head down and not look at Darren. He was very close to me, I could smell the faint, pleasant tang of the soap he uses, and was aware that his dark, good-looking face was getting nearer and nearer my own.

'I don't understand this.' My voice was still uneven.

'None of these dates fit. Some of these envelopes are years older than the letters.'

'What?' He stopped moving towards me and took the letter from my hand. 'Why would Uncle Edward put letters into envelopes that don't belong to them?'

'Maybe it's the envelopes we should be looking at, not the contents,' I said. 'What could the dark horse be – an unusual postmark or a rare stamp perhaps?'

'My God!' He picked up one of the books in the pile. 'Philately! The stamp-collecting books. It was one of his hobbies.'

I was flipping excitedly through the envelopes. 'These all look very old. They could be rare and special and...oh, Darren!'

He looked at my excited face and shining eyes and I really thought he was going to kiss me. 'What is it, Liz?'

I held one out to him, pointing to the stamp with a trembling finger. 'Look at this stamp.'

He did a double-take. 'It's a horse, a black horse!'

'No, not black.' I touched it gently. 'Nearly, but not quite. It's very dark brown. Could it be that *now* you've a dark horse of your own?'

FOURTEEN

DARREN SAT BACK on his heels and let out his breath in a gusty sigh. He was holding the envelope gingerly as though it might suddenly burst into flame.

'I can't believe it's that simple,' he said.

'Simple!' I yelled. 'After all we've been through these last few days you think it's...'

'I know, it's just the letters were the first thing we looked at.'

'The *letters*, yes.' I was collecting the envelopes in a neat bundle. 'But we all read the contents and didn't look at the outside. The stamps are quite dull-looking, you don't even notice the horse one unless you're really peering at it.'

He reached out and took one of the philately books from the bottom of the pile. 'This has been read a few times, that's for sure. It's the sort of thing Uncle Edward would do – put his money into something as obscure as rare stamps. The executors were puzzled by the lack of funds in his estate apparently. He left everything except the desk to charity, but there wasn't the huge amount his solicitors were expecting.'

'Well, there's only one way to find out. Here they all are. We'll have to get an expert to value them.'

Somehow, that sounded quite dull and flat. Colin came back and found us quietly tidying up. I think we were too afraid of another disappointment to rant and rave about the stamps and we told him in a matter-of-fact way about the dates on the letters not matching, and showed him the dark brown horse stamp.

He shook his head, stared at the stamp for a minute or two, then shook his head again. 'D'you really think...let me see the book, please, Darren.' He flipped rapidly through the pages. 'I remember Uncle Edward saying he was going to a high-class stamp auction a few years back. He was full of it at the time, but he didn't ever mention the outcome. I thought philately had been a...passing fancy, as it were.'

'Can you remember when the auction took place?' I said. 'Was it around the time he paid that visit to Tanglewood?'

Colin paused, the open book in his hand. 'I can't...no, hang on, it would have been just after that. He was full of it during his stay, and then as I say, he didn't mention it again. We hardly ever met, as you know, but I used to phone him regularly.'

'What a secretive old devil,' I said. 'He wrote the riddle/ clue just after he came here that time, remember. Darren pinpointed the date when we thought the dark horse meant Toshak.'

'That's *right!*' Colin started his familiar pacing, running his fingers through his hair. 'And if my uncle had just bought the stamps and had tucked them away in the desk it all fits with the *now that you've a dark horse of your own.*'

Darren leapt to his feet and joined in the pacing. He couldn't do the trick with his hair because the hand he uses was the one in the sling, but the two of them looked uncannily like mirror-images.

'Sit down!' I yelled. All that marching up and down was doing my head in. They both looked surprised but they did stop. 'I can't stand any more theorising,' I said firmly. 'Let's find out where you take stamps to be valued, and do it.'

'You're right.' Colin moved across to the phone and started looking through the directories. 'I'll ring round and go.'

'And I'll make a sandwich.' Darren said it with great

importance, then looked down at his one good hand.

'Half a sandwich?' I suggested and we both fell about, feeling suddenly light-hearted again. In the end I made the sandwiches and Colin grabbed one on his way out of the door.

'Found someone,' he said, through a huge mouthful. 'Moortown. I'll be gone all afternoon, unless you both want to come too?'

Darren and I looked at each other. 'Why not?'

We packed the sandwiches and a flask, grabbed some apples and biscuits and ran out to the Land Rover. It felt exciting, like an unexpected picnic, and it felt *urgent* somehow, as if the stamp expert would vanish if we didn't get to Moortown really quickly. We bowled along, Darren and I chatting nonstop except at the point where we left the quiet country road and filtered onto the dual carriageway. The traffic was appalling – heavy lorries, cars and coaches thundering along at a great pace. Our eyes met as we both thought of Toshak and Malachi's fate if they'd reached this stretch just forty-eight hours ago. Darren squeezed my hand gently and didn't let go. I immediately felt wonderful, so happy I was on top of the world.

The morning's competition, proving Ian Daccombe's evil to his father and assuring Tosh's future safety – oh, yes, and the rapidly growing closeness between Darren and me, all combined to make life perfect again. We started singing something from the top ten and it wasn't till I realised Colin wasn't joining in that I looked at him properly. He was concentrating on the road, but his forehead was creased with worry, and the lines round his mouth were cruelly deep. Tanglewood was running out of time and if the stamps proved to be as worthless as the desk, we were back to square one and all out of bright ideas.

The strain was definitely showing. Poor Colin's

determined optimism had been stretched to its limit and I didn't think he could stand another disappointment. Apart from saving his beloved Tanglewood, he felt his own judgment was seen to be at stake. He'd believed in his uncle, believed he had the means and the desire to finance the school's improvements, and to be proved wrong again would seem to him another personal failure. I crossed my fingers on the hand that wasn't enfolded in Darren's and tried to cross my toes too.

We ate the food on the way and drank the coffee in the car park outside the grand-looking building that housed the valuers.

'I've made an appointment.' Colin checked the time. 'Shall we meet up in an hour? There's a great saddlers in the shopping mall – I'll see you there.'

Darren patted his back awkwardly, looking suddenly very serious. 'You'll be all right? Good luck.'

His dad smiled for the first time since we'd left home. 'Thanks, son, I'll be fine.'

We watched him ring the bell on the heavy panelled door, then crossed the road towards the shops. We'd both gone a bit quiet, realising the enormity of the valuers' decision.

'It'll be OK.' I slipped my hand timidly back into Darren's.

His dark eyes looked warmly into mine. 'Sure. D'you know that's the first time you've actually held *my* hand? It's been all me up to now. I was beginning to think you didn't like me.'

'Oh, I like you.' I tried to be flippant. 'I'm just never sure if I'll be welcome. You might have been waiting for a gorgeous blonde to hold your hand.'

'You've got a real hang-up about gorgeous blondes.' He lifted both our hands up and kissed my fingers. 'Or at least about Sasha.'

'I've always thought you'd prefer her,' I said shyly. 'Everyone does.'

'Rubbish. I told you, she's not a patch on you. Do you know what I like most about her?'

'What?' I held my breath, dreading his reply.

'The fact that, like me, she thinks you're the most wonderful thing since sliced bread,' he said, and I knew he meant every word.

I caught sight of our reflections in a shop window as we walked towards the saddlers. We looked great together – we looked *great* together. The hour flew by. I just love looking at things horsey and this was a huge shop with all the up-to-the-minute clothes and accessories as well as the lovely smelling leather in the tack department. I bought Tosh some apple-flavoured horse treats and Darren bought me some new string gloves to replace my disgustingly tatty ones. I then wanted to get him something too, but I had hardly any money left so we shared a Mars Bar and it tasted like nectar and ambrosia.

(All right, I admit I've no idea what they taste like, but I did that day.)

I'd just finished the last mouthful when Darren's hand tightened on mine so sharply I squeaked in pain.

'Sorry.' His eyes were fixed on the door. 'Dad's on his way. I just saw him pass the window.'

We stared at the door and when Colin appeared in it, my heart sank to my boots, I thought he looked so solemn.

'Darren...the stamps...they must be worthless.'

He almost pulled me across the shop. 'It's all right. Look at his face, Liz. *It's all right!*'

And I saw that Colin, now he'd caught sight of us, was beaming, a teeth-showing, face-splitting, ear-to-ear grin of pure delight. We didn't say anything, just fell on each other and all three of us had the biggest hug that the saddlers' shop has ever seen. I had tears streaming down my face and the four dark eyes above me were suspiciously moist-looking. We walked back to the car park, almost floating really, the joy and relief were so euphoric.

'What can I say, Liz?' Colin unlocked the door and we all climbed in. 'You've done it again. Individually those stamps are very rare and worth a bomb, but as a collection they are priceless.'

'Priceless!' Darren and I sounded like a couple of backing singers.

'I've never seen anyone look as excited as that valuer in there. He called in his colleagues, he spoke to other experts on the phone, and he was trembling, actually trembling.'

'Do they know where Uncle Edward got them?' Darren asked. Like me, he was finding it hard to believe that a few old stamps could engender such delirium, let alone such money.

'I told him what I remembered about the auction, gave him the rough date and so on and he got even more gee-ed up. That's when he made his phone calls. The bulk of the collection was bought by my uncle for a pretty astronomical sum at that very sale.'

'When you say the bulk,' I asked, 'which ones weren't bought at the same time?'

'Just the one. The mystery stamp. The 'jewel in the crown' the valuer called it. I won't give you three guesses which...'

'The dark horse,' we both sang out again.

'That one is something utterly fabulous and it really is a mystery where it came from. Anyway, combined with the other collection, the entire staff of valuers say we're talking about a phenomenal sum of money.'

'Enough to pay off the loan?' Darren said anxiously. As I say, it's hard to take in that a few bits of paper can be worth all that.

'Oh, yes. And plenty enough to finance every other improvement we've ever talked or dreamed about.'

'Coooeeee,' I said. 'And I only had just enough for one Mars Bar!'

That set us all giggling and we laughed and sang and talked all the way home – home to our beloved, our forever Tanglewood.

And that's the story. Colin got everything sorted out and I shall start as a working pupil in September. Beech Paddock was kitted out with stout post and rail fencing, too tough for even the largest weasel wielding wire-cutters, and that aforementioned weasel was shipped up North somewhere to be improved under the regime of a very tough military style college. (And he didn't get his sports car. Hah!)

Bill and Wendy and all the staff not only kept their jobs, but were given a handsome 'profit-sharing' bonus, too. Colin threw the most fabulous joint birthday party for Darren and me (same day, I might have mentioned, only he's a year older) and also included Sasha who was sixteen just three days before. Everyone, but everyone joined us. All my family, Mum, Dad, brother, cousins, aunties, even my *nan* mingling happily with Darren's mates from school. Loads of Sasha's and my friends came too and it was brilliant. Of course, being Sasha, the first thing she did was to bring her mum over to meet Colin.

Her mum is divorced, very sweet, and extremely attractive and I have the feeling her daughter has marked Colin down as an eligible proposition for her.

'He's much too nice to stay a widower for ever,' Sasha confided in me. 'And he'd be so much happier with a good woman. I mean – look at Darren.'

I pulled her nose and she pretended to ruffle up my scrunch-dried, trendily messy hair. I was wearing a fabulous new skirt and top my mum had bought for my birthday, though at first I wasn't sure what Darren thought of this new image – then he told me I was the most beautiful girl in the room, and for the first time in my life I felt I was.

We danced and talked and laughed all night, and when the last guests had left, he took my hand and walked me home in the moonlight. The stars were dancing too, high in an indigo heaven, and the air was full of summer fragrance. Darren stopped under the branches of a sweet chestnut tree and lifted my face up to his. He stroked my hair softly and at last his lips were touching mine – or was it part of my dream, that birthday night?

I can be a bit of a dark horse myself sometimes – you'll never know, will you?